D. Larry Crumbley, PhD, CPA
Shelton Taxation Professor

Texas A&M University
College Station, Texas

and

Jack P. Friedman, PhD, CPA
College Station, Texas

D1714259

BA

New York • Lond

ACKNOWLEDGMENTS

The authors are grateful to Eric J. Kohn, tax collection consultant, and Edmund Nowicki, tax attorney, for their careful review and valuable suggestions. Howell Lynch, Virginia A. Nichols, and Lisa Rivers also provided valuable input.

All inquiries should be addressed to:
Barron's Educational Series, Inc.
250 Wireless Boulevard
Hauppauge, New York 11788

Library of Congress Catalog Card No. 90-23550

International Standard Book No. 0-8120-4513-0

Library of Congress Cataloging in Publication Data

Crumbley, D. Larry.
  Keys to surviving a tax audit / by D. Larry Crumbley and Jack P. Friedman.
    p. cm.—(Barron's business keys)
  Includes index.
  ISBN 0-8120-4513-0
  1. Tax auditing—United States.   2. United States. Internal Revenue Service.   I. Friedman, Jack P.   II. Title.   III. Series.
KF6314.C78 1991
343.7304—dc20   90-23550
[347.3034]   CIP

PRINTED IN THE UNITED STATES OF AMERICA
1234 5500 987654321

CONTENTS

1

PURPOSE OF THIS BOOK

In 1913, U.S. Representative Cordell Hull said that "every citizen should be willing to devote a brief time during some one day in the year, when necessary, to the making up of a listing of his income for taxes."

Today, few people can avoid confronting the income tax, whether an individual paying for government services or a businessman concerned with a significant expense in his enterprise. You should pay what is legally due but not a dollar more, and it is likely that your payment could be reduced if you plan and organize. Planning purposefully and keeping records effectively will help you in nontax ways, also. The days when the average tax return could be prepared in a "brief time" on "one day in the year" are long past.

The Internal Revenue Service collects an astonishing amount of money each year. In 1989, the IRS's gross collections exceeded $1 trillion. About $515 billion of that came from the more than 110 million individual tax returns processed by the IRS.

The percentage of individual tax returns that the IRS audits has decreased since 1970. But that is no consolation if yours is among the approximately one million selected for audit each year. An accurate return, honest preparation, a good recordkeeping system, and some luck can reduce the fear and consequences of an IRS audit.

The IRS does not punish tax offenders with public floggings, as did ancient Egyptian bureaucrats. Instead, it relies on an array of civil and criminal penalties to encourage payment. With the authority to collect interest on any amount due, and more than 150 penalties at its disposal, the IRS is a formidable adversary. In *A Law Unto Itself* (Random House, 1991), David Burnham describes the IRS as "the single most powerful instrument of social control in the country."

This book is intended to serve as a guide to reducing your chances of an IRS audit. If an audit does occur, this book will help arm you with the knowledge, strength, and information needed to survive the process. A better understanding of taxation can prevent the all-too-common belief that we are born free and taxed to death.

2

SOURCES OF THE TAX LAWS

The most important source of tax law is the Internal Revenue Code. The present code, the Internal Revenue Code of 1986, contains thousands of sections that have been painstakingly assembled and reassembled by legislators over the last half-century.

Tax laws begin as revenue bills in the House of Representatives. These bills originate in various ways. For example, the President may make a proposal or recommendation in the annual budget message to Congress or in the State of the Union address. The proposal is turned over to the Ways and Means Committee of the House of Representatives.

The proposed tax laws are considered carefully by members before the Ways and Means Committee. Frequently, representatives of the Treasury Department and the staff of the Joint Committee on Internal Revenue Taxation—which consists of members of both the House Ways and Means Committee and the Senate Finance Committee—are invited to sit in on the deliberations. On significant proposals, public hearings are held. After these hearings, the Ways and Means Committee retires into executive session. The committee then proposes a bill, which is passed on to the entire House of Representatives. If approved by the full House, the bill goes to the Senate Finance Committee.

The bill, with any amendments from the Senate Finance Committee, is then presented on the floor of the Senate, where further amendments may be proposed. The bill passed by the Senate may be quite different from the one passed by the House. If so, a conference committee, consisting of five members from both houses, may try to reach a compromise. Both houses then vote on the final version and, if it is accepted by a majority, send it to the President for approval.

Under the Constitution, the President has ten days (excluding Sundays) from the day it is presented to him to sign the bill into law. If he vetoes the bill during that period, it is returned to Congress. There the President's veto may be overridden by a two-thirds majority in both houses. If the President takes no action during the ten-day period, the bill becomes law without his signature. But if Congress adjourns in the meantime, the bill dies. This is called a pocket veto.

When a bill is sent to the floor by a congressional committee, it is usually accompanied by a committee report. That report includes significant facts behind the bill, the reason it has been proposed, and its probable effect on government revenues and on taxpayers. A conference committee may also issue a report, although this report may be merely a summary of the bill's evolution. The reports of the Ways and Means Committee and the Senate Finance Committee are public documents, valuable in understanding tax legislation and *congressional intent.*

Of course, not all tax bills progress in exactly this fashion. However, once a bill becomes law, it changes the Internal Revenue Code.

3

GRAY AREAS

There are "gray areas" in the tax law. In other
words, not all tax issues are clearly addressed by
the Internal Revenue Code. Consider, for example,
a certain expenditure to alter part of a rental building. Is it a deductible repair expense or a capital
improvement? The answer to this question may turn
on whether the life of the building will be prolonged,
which may be a matter of opinion. Questions like
these usually result in a substantial number of IRS-
taxpayer confrontations.

Even IRS personnel don't always have definitive
answers. However, the IRS must follow its own
published position in regulations, revenue rulings,
etc., even though another answer may be more correct. The IRS admits that its employees responded
incorrectly to more than a third of the questions
that taxpayers asked over the phone in 1989. So
beware of answers from the IRS. If your tax practitioner and the IRS give you different answers to
a question, don't assume that the practitioner is
wrong. In the North Atlantic region, callers to the
IRS had a 59 percent chance of getting the wrong
answer to a question about capital gains in 1989.

If you contact the IRS for information, make
notes of whom you spoke or corresponded with,
questions you asked, and the replies you received.
You may be able to avoid a penalty for following
bad advice, especially if the IRS published it.

For several years, *Money* magazine has asked fifty
tax professionals to calculate the tax liability of a

hypothetical family. Each year these experts have come up with different answers. One year the correct answer was $12,038, and the experts' answers ranged from $9,806 to $21,315. There was no clear correlation between the fees charged and accuracy. Incidentally, over the past three years the average preparation fee has risen 30 percent.

As *Money* magazine points out, if our complicated tax code can trip up even highly trained CPAs, what hope does a mere layman have unless his return is relatively simple or he is an avid amateur accountant willing to put in long hours of study?

Fortunately, most controversies are settled at the IRS level or just before going to court. But even the relatively few that go to court result in a huge volume of litigation and published court opinions. Often, even published opinions differ on a certain tax issue, as noted in Key 46.

4

TAX AVOIDANCE VS. TAX EVASION

Legally permitted tax reduction methods constitute tax *avoidance*. Tax *evasion* is any method of reducing taxes not permitted by law. Avoidance is playing the game according to the rules. Evasion is breaking the rules—*a criminal offense* that carries heavy penalties.

Tax avoiders do not conceal or misrepresent; rather, they shape events and transactions to reduce or eliminate tax liability. For example, you write a check and send it to a charity on December 30 to obtain a charitable-contribution deduction for the year just ending. Although the payment is for next year's dues and the check is not cashed until January 20, the deduction is considered applicable to the previous year. (Taxpayers should be aware, however, that prepayment of a tax-deductible item is not always deductible in the year paid.) Another example of tax avoidance is purchasing tax-exempt municipal bonds instead of fully taxable corporate bonds.

Tax evasion, by contrast, involves attempts to conceal or obscure. For example, a taxpayer writes a check for a charitable contribution on December 30 but does not mail the check until January 5. Or the taxpayer writes the check in January and puts a December date on it. Other examples of tax evasion are knowingly reporting 200 miles of travel on a business trip instead of the correct mileage of

120, and claiming restaurant dinners with a personal friend as a business expense. Of course, failing to report income is also tax evasion. In 1990, Pete Rose admitted that he had failed to report $354,968 in income from autograph appearances, memorabilia sales, and gambling. (Yes, even income earned illegally is taxable.)

Most tax evasion schemes fall into one of the following categories:

(a) Understatement or omission of income.
(b) Claiming fictitious or improper deductions.
(c) False allocation of income.
(d) Improper claims for credit or exemption.

Even laudable motives are no defense. For example, a taxpayer may intentionally understate income to have sufficient money to support parents who are invalids. Although the motive is admirable, it is still tax evasion in the eyes of the IRS.

The IRS imposes civil and criminal sanctions against tax law violators. It adds civil penalties to the tax liability, but they are not considered felonies (i.e., criminal violations). See Keys 28 and 29.

Most criminal sanctions involve imprisonment, fines, or both. For example, a taxpayer who attempts in any manner to evade or defeat a tax may be fined not more than $100,000, imprisoned not more than five years, or both. In addition, the convicted taxpayer must pay court costs.

Both civil and criminal sanctions may be imposed for the same offense. The difference often is a matter of whether the IRS wants to make a public example out of a particular tax evader, simply collect the money, or both. Generally, the IRS prefers just to collect the tax plus any noncriminal penalties the law permits, even though the taxpayer could be prosecuted for a criminal offense.

Three elements are necessary for an action to be

considered criminal: (1) an additional tax is due, (2) an attempt is made in any manner to evade or defeat the tax, and (3) the attempt is willful. The IRS must prove every facet of the offense and show guilt beyond a reasonable doubt. When seeking a fraud conviction, the IRS has the burden of establishing fraud by clear and convincing evidence. A taxpayer will be acquitted if the evidence is as consistent with innocence as with guilt.

The IRS must establish that, at the time the offense was committed, an additional tax was due and owing. But the IRS does not have to prove evasion of the full amount, only that a substantial amount of the tax was evaded. This proof need not be in terms of gross or net income or a percentage of the tax shown to be due and payable. It is current IRS policy not to assess any additional taxes and penalties while criminal charges are pending and to postpone any discussion or negotiation involving settlement of the civil liability.

The phrase "attempt in any manner" implies that the crime occurs when the attempt is made, whether it succeeds or fails. The criminal nature of an offense lies not in the failure to file a return or in the filing of a false return, but rather in the *attempt* to evade a tax.

The Supreme Court has given the following examples of conduct from which the attempt to evade taxes may be inferred: keeping a double set of books, making false entries, altering invoices or documents, destroying books and records, concealing assets or covering up sources of income, and the handling of one's affairs to avoid making the usual records.

Pete Rose, for example, sold the baseball bat that he used to set the record for most career hits. Rose had the buyer pay him with several checks for

$10,000 or less. Rose must have been confused about the requirement that banks report to the IRS *cash* (not check) transactions of more than $10,000.

A *willful* act is defined as one undertaken with a bad purpose; without justifiable excuse; or stubbornly, obstinately, or perversely. The Supreme Court has decreed that *willful* characterizes an act done without grounds for believing it is lawful, or conduct marked by careless disregard as to whether or not one has the right to so act.

Willfulness is a state of mind and is thus difficult to prove. Courts have deemed that the following acts prove willfulness: attempting to bribe a revenue agent, entering undisclosed safe-deposit boxes after having been questioned about assets, making false statements, withholding records during investigation, and influencing the testimony of a prospective witness.

5

PURPOSE OF
THE IRS

The Internal Revenue Service, also called the "IRS" or "Service," is the branch of the Treasury Department that administers the federal income tax. Its chief officer is the commissioner of internal revenue, who is appointed by the President of the United States.

The stated purpose of the IRS is to collect the proper amount of tax revenue at the least cost to the public and in a manner that warrants the highest degree of public confidence in its integrity, efficiency, and fairness.

If you were in charge of the IRS, how would you want the public to think of it? As a tough and stubborn agency, or as a pushover that any aggressive taxpayer can take advantage of? Once you answer that question—and recognize that Congress puts the IRS on a limited budget to get the greatest collections at the lowest cost—you'll understand why the IRS conducts itself as it does.

The IRS is also charged with the following:
- encouraging and achieving the highest possible degree of voluntary compliance with the tax law and regulations;
- advising the public of their rights and responsibilities;
- determining the extent of compliance and the causes of noncompliance;

- doing what is needed for the proper administration and enforcement of the tax laws;
- continually searching for and implementing new, more efficient and effective ways of accomplishing its mission.

At the end of the fiscal year 1989, the IRS had more than 114,500 employees, about 600 domestic offices, and more than a dozen offices abroad. It spent $5.2 billion to administer the nation's tax system. It received 199.6 million tax returns and other related documents, collected $921.5 billion in taxes, and issued nearly 92 million refunds. In addition, the IRS assisted tens of millions of taxpayers through a variety of programs.

The IRS's headquarters is in Washington, D.C. However, individual taxpayers are seldom in contact with this office. The IRS partitions the country into seven regions, each supervised by a regional commissioner. There are ten regional service centers, to which tax returns are mailed by taxpayers. They are located in the following cities:

Andover, Massachusetts 05501
Atlanta, Georgia 39901
Austin, Texas 73301
Cincinnati, Ohio 45999
Fresno, California 93888
Holtsville, New York 00501
Kansas City, Missouri 64999
Memphis, Tennessee 37501
Ogden, Utah 84201
Philadelphia, Pennsylvania 19255

Regions are divided into districts, each run by a district director. Contact between taxpayers and the IRS—such as for audits—is usually through district offices.

6

IRS DIVISIONS

The enforcement arm of the Internal Revenue Service is composed of three main divisions: Examination, Collection, and Criminal Investigation. The Examination and Collection Divisions have jurisdiction in civil matters, whereas criminal liability is the province of the Criminal Investigation Division.

The Examination Division determines whether a taxpayer has properly reported income. If an IRS examination results in an assessment of additional taxes or penalties, the case is turned over to the Collection Division.

The Collection Division attempts to collect delinquent accounts. It might attach a taxpayer's salary, bank account, or other source of income. It may seize and sell homes, cars, business assets, or other property. (For example, in 1990 the IRS filed a $16.7 million lien on property owned by entertainer Willie Nelson.) It may also investigate taxpayers who fail to file required returns, and may assist special agents of the Criminal Investigation Division.

Suspected fraud is handled by the Criminal Investigation Division (CID). The CID is a highly trained organization of 2,800 special agents, most of whom are accountants or attorneys. Criminal aspects of tax law violations are of concern to the CID, especially criminal activity in the areas of individual and corporate income taxes, withholding, excise, and other taxes. Violations of related tax statutes and the Bank Secrecy Act also come under the CID's purview. CID special agents make recommendations and provide assistance for criminal prosecution and for assessment of civil penalties. They testify in court as government witnesses.

CID special agents also serve as financial experts in the Organized Crime Drug Enforcement Task Forces. This program was instituted in 1982 to identify, investigate, and prosecute members of drug-trafficking enterprises. Thirteen task forces throughout the United States combine the expertise of the Federal Bureau of Investigation, Drug Enforcement Administration, Bureau of Alcohol, Tobacco and Firearms, and U.S. Customs Service. CID special agents play an important role because of their ability to determine an individual's net worth and to identify the schemes used by drug traffickers to disguise asset ownership.

The CID also cooperates with the Justice Department in the Federal Organized Strike Force Program, which is directed at organized crime. The CID is able to secure indictments for tax violations against otherwise untouchable criminals.

7

TYPES OF IRS EMPLOYEES

In this key, the most common occupations within the IRS are described.

Extractors remove tax returns from envelopes and sort them according to whether payment is enclosed.

Return analysis staff members review tax returns for completeness. They check for signatures and missing schedules and compare the amounts written on checks to the amounts stated on the tax returns.

Classifiers/screeners are experienced auditors on temporary assignment who review tax returns to eliminate any that are not audit candidates. The remaining returns are sent back to the service center highlighted with issues to be audited. These people eyeball returns and consider attachments or explanations that computers cannot process.

Tax examiners are taxpayers' first point of contact with the IRS. Examiners handle correspondence audits.

Tax auditors are members of the Examination Division (see Key 6) who audit simple, nonbusiness returns, usually at an IRS office. A tax auditor does not necessarily have a college degree in accounting. Although the scope of the examination is established by the *classifier checklist,* which lists items that warrant examination, tax auditors may expand the scope on the basis of information secured during the examination.

Revenue agents are also members of the Examination Division. They audit complicated and problematic individual and business returns, usually at the taxpayer's home or office. Revenue agents set the scope of the examination; they have authority to expand or restrict audits as circumstances warrant. A revenue agent has a college degree in accounting.

Special agents are members of the Criminal Investigation Division of the IRS (see Key 6) who seek to develop criminal cases against taxpayers. Special agents aim their efforts at programs such as organized crime, narcotics, money laundering, questionable refund schemes, illegal tax shelters, and other domestic and international violations. Special agents recommend criminal prosecution in a variety of industries and occupations.

Revenue officers are members of the IRS's Collection Division (see Key 6). They go to taxpayers' homes or businesses to collect delinquent taxes and tax returns. Although voluntary payments are encouraged, revenue officers are authorized to use seizures, levies, distraints, and other involuntary procedures to exact payment.

Each IRS district, service center, and regional office has a *problem resolution officer* (PRO). In resolving taxpayers' problems and protecting their rights, PROs may intervene in situations where IRS action or inaction would cause a hardship for the taxpayer. See Keys 26 and 41.

8

TYPES OF
TAXPAYERS

There is an old joke that a taxpayer is someone who doesn't have to take a civil service exam to work for the government.

The Internal Revenue Code defines a *taxpayer* as any person or entity subject to an internal revenue tax. This definition encompasses individuals, corporations, partnerships, trusts, estates, joint-stock companies, associations, and syndicates. It also encompasses guardians, committees, trustees, executors, administrators, trustees in bankruptcy, receivers, and assignees.

Most individuals have little trouble choosing the right tax return. But problems often arise in this area for artificial entities such as trusts, estates, partnerships, and corporations. Almost all income tax returns fall into one of the following five categories:

Type of Return	Form	Filed by
Individual	1040, 1040A 1040EZ	Every natural person with income in excess of the statutory minimum
Corporation	1120	Corporations, including organizations taxed as corporations
S Corporation	1120S	Corporations taxed as partnerships
Fiduciary	1041	Trusts and estates with income in excess of statutory minimums
Partnership	1065	Partnerships or joint ventures (information returns only)

All taxpaying entities are subject to the IRS's audit mechanism. This book emphasizes the audit of individual taxpayers.

9

SELF-ASSESSMENT

One of the underlying principles of tax law in the United States is self-assessment. Self-assessment means that every person must determine whether he or she is obligated to file a tax return. If so, it is the person's responsibility to file a tax return and to comply with the law regarding payment.

Your employer must give you at least two copies of Form W-2 by January 31. Other parties send you information returns such as Form 1099 for interest, dividends, and other types of income. When you receive these forms, gather all pertinent information and prepare a tax return as soon as possible. Why the rush? First, this gives you more time to seek any information that may be missing. Second, and perhaps more important, you may have a refund coming. A refund received today is worth more than the same amount received three or four months from now. By contrast, if you owe the IRS money, you will probably want to delay mailing your return until the last possible moment.

Filing a tax return on time and paying any taxes owed does not necessarily discharge your obligation. After filing a tax return, you may find that you erred in some way in the procedure. For example, perhaps you inadvertently omitted a Form 1099 amount or neglected to declare a charitable contribution. To correct such an omission, you can voluntarily file Form 1040X to amend the return; your payment will stop penalties and interest from mounting. However, the likelihood of an audit will increase (see Key 19).

The American system of income taxation may be based on self-assessment and voluntary compliance, but the government has found that a system of enforcement is necessary to protect its revenue. Our tax system is not truly voluntary, because legally you *must* report your income and may incur both civil and criminal penalties for failure to do so.

10

THE BURDEN FALLS
ON YOU

In nearly all tax disputes, the burden of proof falls on the taxpayer. In effect, this means you are guilty until proven innocent. Therefore, it is essential that you keep good tax records. Besides, organization and preparation can reduce taxes.

All taxpayers whose income exceeds a certain dollar amount must maintain accounting records—books of account and other records and data as may be necessary to support entries on the tax return. The law does not specify the type of records taxpayers should maintain. The system should record income when it is received and payments for deductible expenses as they are made. Sales slips, bills, invoices, receipts, canceled checks, and other documents may be used to support tax deductions. Dates of sale and purchase of real estate and other investments can be important because of long-term and short-term calculations.

A taxpayer whose sole source of income is wages need not keep formal accounting books. Copies of tax returns, W-2 forms, and other information returns are usually sufficient to establish the method used to prepare the income tax return. Invoices with canceled checks are usually adequate to substantiate deductions.

Failure to keep adequate records may increase your tax liability or result in a penalty. The U.S. Tax Court sustained a negligence penalty (see Key

28) against one taxpayer who claimed certain business deductions but did not have the necessary documents to back them up. The taxpayer had maintained only a partial log for the business expenses, and some of the expenses were "questionable."

Tax returns and most tax records should be retained for at least seven years. Reference to old tax returns can greatly simplify preparation of a current return. Some records should be kept longer than seven years, such as those for home purchase and home improvement expenditures, retirement plan contributions, and assets that you are depreciating. And some records should be kept indefinitely—the records that prove the tax basis of any assets you hold, for example.

11

RECORDKEEPING SUGGESTIONS

If you are a typical taxpayer, you spend approximately a third of your working hours earning money just to pay taxes. In fact, sometimes it seems you have to earn your money twice—once from your job or business and again in the effort required to avoid paying more tax than necessary. One way to reduce your tax obligation is to keep good, accurate records to substantiate legitimate deductions.

Maintaining organized tax records is not difficult. First, you need an accurate checkbook and check register. Second, you have to organize receipts and other paper records in files or envelopes. Third, you need some way of summarizing your annual income and expenses. Several computer programs are now available for that purpose.

Use checks to pay bills, especially those for tax-deductible items. A canceled check is evidence of payment that can be used during an audit. On each check note what you are paying—for example, "charitable contribution," or "federal income tax payment for 1990 Form 1040." Write clearly in your check register, and place a mark next to those payments that are tax deductible. This procedure will help you identify deductible items when you begin preparing your tax return.

Before the start of each year, buy a set of folders, envelopes, or files to help organize all those loose scraps of paper you will receive. Label each folder with the year and account or purpose of the expenditure, such as "Charitable Contributions—1991," for example. Use different colors for different years; this can help prevent filing errors. And be sure to mark each bill you pay with the date and check number. This will help you find things quickly when tax time comes.

Summarize the year's financial activity using a pad with columns (devoting each column on the pad to a different expense category), spreadsheet computer program, or packaged personal financial computer program. Such a system may help you in nontax matters, such as locating a receipt to back up a warranty or submitting an insurance claim. It may also help you manage your budgeting and investing activities.

Keep a record of large or unusual transactions, even those that have no immediate tax significance. For example, if your aunt Leah gives you a $500 birthday present, be sure to note the gift in your records. If you give $5,000 in cash to your favorite charity, get a receipt. A canceled check by itself does not prove you made a contribution. The IRS is on the watch for those seemingly generous donors who receive "change" in return for their large contributions. If you give property to charity, keep a record of the property's valuation appraisal.

Use a diary or log to note car mileage and transportation expenses spent for business, medical, and charitable purposes. Do you entertain clients? If so, it is good policy to pay with a credit card and write the clients' names and the purpose of your business or subject of discussion on your receipt. An IRS auditor may ask to see your diary or day timer to match appointments with deductions. For example, an auditor may take note that you did no traveling on a day when an ice storm or blizzard shut down all roads in the area. In this way, your recordkeeping helps to increase the credibility of your deductions.

IRS Publication 552 describes recordkeeping requirements for individuals; Publication 583 is for businesses.

12

HELP FROM THE IRS

You can get plenty of tax help from the IRS. Publication 910, *Guide to Free Tax Services,* is a catalog of IRS publications and services. *Your Federal Income Tax* (#17), *Your Rights As a Taxpayer* (#1), *Tax Guide for Small Business* (#334), and *Business Reporting* (#937) are especially helpful publications. There is a list of IRS publications at the end of this key. You should keep in mind, however, that a lot of information provided by the IRS is not reliable or correct (see Key 3).

The IRS provides three kinds of telephone assistance lines for taxpayers: (1) a toll-free system with trained staff to help with technical tax law, procedural questions, and account problems; (2) Tele-Tax, for either recorded technical tax law information or the status of the current year's refund; and, (3) a special toll-free number—1-800-424-FORM (3676)—for taxpayers to use to order forms and publications. Phone numbers to call from your area for technical assistance and Tele-Tax are listed in *Your Federal Income Tax.*

Tele-Tax provides recorded tax information on approximately 140 tax topics. Topics include tax assistance for the handicapped or hearing-impaired, tax fraud, electronic filing, estimated taxes, tip income, and alimony paid. You dial a toll-free number and select the topic or topics you wish to hear.

In 1989, the IRS began offering additional walk-in offices and extended hours, including Saturdays and limited hours on Sundays. Some areas offer a math verification program to help taxpayers. The IRS also uses computer programs to review returns, identify errors, and provide on-the-spot corrections.

Also in 1989, the IRS initiated "One-Stop Service," a program designed to help taxpayers meet their tax obligations through a single IRS contact. Districts resolve account problems while talking to the taxpayer. Several districts also invited state tax agencies to join the IRS at tax-preparation sites.

Two IRS-sponsored programs use trained volunteers at community sites to help special groups of taxpayers—including the low-income, non-English-speaking, handicapped, and elderly—fill out their tax returns. In 1989, the Volunteer Income Tax Assistance (VITA) program helped about a million taxpayers, and the Tax Counseling for the Elderly (TCE) program helped over 1.3 million.

Taxpayers who wish to avail themselves of VITA should bring a current package of tax return forms, wage-and-earnings statements (Form W-2) from all employers, information returns (Form 1099), a copy of last year's tax return (if available), and any other relevant information. However, VITA does not get involved in complicated tax matters.

Community Outreach Tax Assistance provides tax assistance and information to more than a million taxpayers. This program is offered at times and locations convenient for taxpayers who are unable to seek help at IRS offices during normal business hours.

Photocopies of your old income tax returns can be obtained from the IRS for $4.25 each, although there is a six-week wait. There is no charge for a transcript of individual tax account information. To make these requests, complete Form 4506, Request for Copy of Tax Form, and mail it and prepayment to the address shown on the form.

Requests for IRS tax forms and publications should be sent to a forms distribution center at one of the following addresses:

Rancho Cordova, CA 95743–0001: Alaska, Arizona, California, Colorado, Hawaii, Idaho, Montana, Nevada, New Mexico, Oregon, Utah, Washington, Wyoming.

P.O. Box 9903, Bloomington, IL 61799: Alabama, Arkansas, Illinois, Indiana, Iowa, Kansas, Kentucky, Louisiana, Michigan, Minnesota, Mississippi, Missouri, Nebraska, North Dakota, Ohio, Oklahoma, South Dakota, Tennessee, Texas, Wisconsin.

P.O. Box 25866, Richmond, VA 23289: Connecticut, Delaware, District of Columbia, Florida, Georgia, Maine, Maryland, Massachusetts, New Hampshire, New Jersey, New York, North Carolina, Pennsylvania, Rhode Island, South Carolina, Vermont, Virginia, West Virginia.

General Guides

- 1 Your Rights as a Taxpayer
- 2 The ABC's of Income Tax
- 17 Your Federal Income Tax
- 225 Farmer's Tax Guide
- 334 Tax Guide for Small Business
- 509 Tax Calendars for 1990
- 553 Highlights of 1989 Tax Changes
- 595 Tax Guide for Commercial Fishermen
- 910 Guide to Free Tax Services

Specialized Publications

- 3 Tax Information for Military Personnel
- 4 Student's Guide to Federal Income Tax
- 15 Employer's Tax Guide (Circular E)
- 54 Tax Guide for U.S. Citizens and Resident Aliens Abroad

13

TYPES OF TAX PREPARERS

For most people, preparing a tax return is a difficult and tedious chore. In fact, many people believe that it is impossible to comply with tax laws without assistance from trained preparers. There are five main types of tax preparers: tax attorneys, certified public accountants (CPAs), enrolled agents, chain-store tax preparers, and unenrolled tax preparers.

Tax attorneys are often consulted in matters that require intricate knowledge of the law. Some tax attorneys have spent a year or more after law school to receive a master's degree in taxation; some are also CPAs. Most tax attorneys charge more than other types of preparers.

CPAs are authorized to represent taxpayers before all administrative levels of the IRS. They have passed a rigorous twenty-hour examination and completed a college degree, including many hours of accounting courses. In most states, CPAs must attend courses each year to retain certification. There are six major CPA firms (the "Big Six") and many medium-size and small ones. CPAs generally work on complex and business tax returns. In addition, many provide tax planning. Most CPAs charge fees based on the time spent on the tax return—between $50 and $200 per hour.

Enrolled agents have passed a two-day IRS exam or have worked in certain capacities at the IRS for at least five years. Like CPAs, they are authorized to represent taxpayers before the IRS. Many of these agents are qualified to complete complex individual tax returns, and their fees may be as high as those of CPAs.

Chain-store franchises, such as H&R Block, hire part-time employees who may have accounting or tax experience. These employees are trained in-house to offer quick and inexpensive service. Consequently, their services tend to be impersonal—most offer no tax planning, for example. However, there are exceptions. For example, the H&R Block Executive Tax Service caters to a more demanding clientele at higher fees.

There are tax preparers who are not licensed CPAs or enrolled agents. They may be full-time tax preparers or moonlight during tax season. They need not have an accounting or tax degree. Most of these preparers charge fees based on time or assignment, and the fees may approach the amount charged by smaller CPA firms. Some states have registration, licensing, or examination requirements for this type of preparer.

Be careful in selecting a tax preparer. If the IRS suspects that a preparer is cheating the government, all of the preparer's returns will be examined for possible audit. Avoid any preparer who guarantees a refund or tells you something that seems too good to be true. For example, one preparer in New York showed his clients one return with no refund due, but mailed to the IRS a different return calling for a tax refund to be mailed to him.

Never sign a blank tax return and leave it with a preparer. You are responsible for whatever is or is not on it.

14

TAX RETURN APPEARANCE

Your tax return should be neat and professional-looking. This gives the IRS reviewer the impression that you are a precise and careful taxpayer. Neat supporting schedules and comments tell an IRS reviewer that you maintain detailed, organized records. For example, if you claim a casualty loss as a result of a flood, a copy of a newspaper report detailing the flooding in your area not only backs up your claim but also shows that you are conscientious and thorough.

A neat and thoroughly prepared tax return reduces your chances of being audited. Missing forms, incomplete schedules, and incorrect forms increase the likelihood that a computer will catch you or that a reviewer will decide to audit you. Complete all the schedules required and double- and triple-check your return.

Be careful to list income on your tax return from all third-party sources, and spell all names correctly. Even when income is listed, the return may be snagged by the IRS's Document Matching Program if the third-party is mislabeled. (See Key 19.) For example, suppose you own stock in IBM that is held in your broker's name. The broker sends you a 1099 to report the dividends, which you declare under "dividends" on your tax return as received from IBM. The IRS may send you a notice that you failed to report income from the broker. You could have avoided that problem by listing the earnings under the broker's name.

Use Form 8822 to notify the IRS if your address changes. In 1989, more than $400 million in refund checks were returned to the IRS by the post office because of changed addresses.

Be sure you (and your spouse if you are filing a joint return) sign your tax return and include a check if money is due the IRS. The check should be written in the amount of the tax liability shown on the return. Write your social security number on the check, and indicate the type of tax being paid (e.g., "1991 Form 1040").

15

TAX RETURN
ROUTE

The process a tax return goes through from the time it comes in the door at an IRS service center until it is filed away is called the "pipeline" (see Exhibit 1, page 35). Extractors remove tax returns from the envelopes and hand-sort them according to whether or not payment is enclosed. Returns with payments are set aside temporarily so that the payments may be recorded. Checks are deposited in the U.S. Treasury.

Next, a document locator number is stamped on each tax return, check, and other documents. Tax returns are then sorted by type, assigned identification numbers, and placed in batches of 100 for data processing. Each return is then checked for completeness and accuracy and coded for computer input. Next, information from the return is entered into a computer network, verified, and recorded on magnetic tape for further processing.

Computers check the mathematical accuracy of all returns and verify all identification numbers. Returns with errors are identified, reviewed, corrected, and re-inputted. Magnetic tapes of tax information are shipped to the National Computer Center in Martinsburg, West Virginia, for posting to a master file. Returns are kept in the Center's files for several months before being shipped to federal record centers.

Since 1967, computers have been used to select

Exhibit 1
The Pipeline

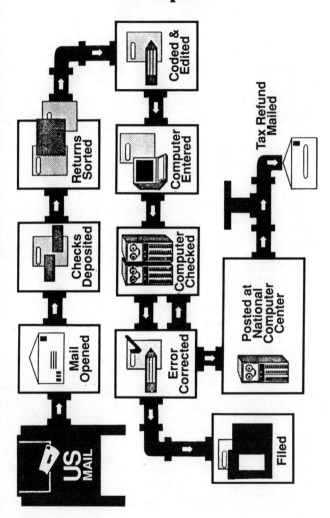

returns to be examined, or "classified for examination," as the IRS terms it. In 1969, a "discriminant function" technique was introduced to facilitate the selection of certain individual returns for audit. See Key 21.

16

OBTAINING REFUNDS FROM THE IRS

A taxpayer who has filed a return with the IRS might be entitled to a tax refund. This refund may be claimed on an original return or on an amended return.

With the IRS's Tele-Tax system, retrieving a current year's refund is a simple process. Tele-Tax is an automated service that taxpayers can use to find out the status of a refund. Using a touch-tone phone, you enter your social security number, your filing status, and the exact amount of the anticipated refund.

If Tele-Tax responds that a check was mailed on a certain date but you don't get it within thirty days from that date, you can report the problem to the nearest taxpayer assistance office. Form 3911 will be sent for you to fill out and return to the IRS so that the matter can be researched. If there is a mistake on the return, Tele-Tax will identify it. The refund check will then be mailed, along with an explanation of any change in the refund amount. As a last resort for obtaining a refund check, you should call the problem resolution officer at the district office where the return was filed. See Key 41.

An amended claim for a refund must be filed at an IRS service center. You can use the forms designated for such a claim (1040X, 1120X, and 843), or otherwise provide the IRS with all pertinent information. The claim should be in writing, state the years for which the claim is sought, and clearly detail the basis for a refund. It is not necessary to state the exact amount of the refund sought. You can state a minimal amount, with a rider adding "or such greater amount as may be legally refundable." The claim can be amended to clarify or add information after it is filed. If the IRS disallows the claim or does not respond within six months from the day the claim is filed, you may bring a refund suit. In most circumstances, you have two years from the time a claim is formally disallowed to bring suit.

17

INTEREST ON DEFICIENCIES AND OVERPAYMENTS

Always file your tax return when it is due (or file for an extension), even when you don't have cash to pay any taxes you owe. You may be able to arrange with the IRS to pay taxes later. If you don't pay the tax on time, interest and certain penalties on the tax begin accruing from the day it is due. Even if you file for an extension of time, interest is due on any unpaid amount that you owe starting on April 15.

On the other hand, you may make an overpayment to the IRS. If that happens, the government must pay you interest if your refund is not mailed within forty-five days from April 15 or the date you file your return (whichever is later). If the IRS misses this deadline, it owes you interest from April 15 *or* from the date on which you filed your late return (provided you have been granted an extension).

The IRS pays you 1 percent less than the rate that you have to pay them. Rates are based on the federal short-term rate, an average market yield of Treasury bills and other U.S. obligations with terms of three years or less. If the IRS owes you, it pays you the short-term rate plus 2 percent (called the *statutory rate*). Yet you must pay the IRS the short-term rate plus 3 percent (called the *assessed interest*). These rates (now approximately 11 to 12 percent) are computed daily and are adjusted quarterly.

Interest paid to you by the IRS is taxable income, and an IRS computer will check to make sure you declare it on your tax return the following year. Any IRS interest that you pay is considered personal interest, and as such is partially deductible. After 1990, however, this interest will not be deductible at all.

Interest is also imposed on penalties and additional tax when these are not paid within ten days from the date of notice and demand. In many cases, interest starts accruing from the date of notice and demand to the date of payment. Since the rate is compounded daily, the interest due can be significant. Certain penalties are assessed as of the due date of the return, and interest accrues from that date.

Calculation of the interest rate—what the IRS pays and what you pay—is exceedingly complex. In 1975, the rate of computation was changed for the first time in forty years, but there have been at least nineteen other changes since that time. The IRS uses computers to make these calculations.

The amount on which quarterly interest is computed is called the *base*. A separate interest computation is needed for each part of an underpayment or overpayment that has a different interest period.

How do you minimize the interest payment? Obviously, paying a deficiency stops interest from accruing. Also, interest stops accumulating while your tax deficiency is being contested if the remittance is a deposit (cash bond) or a payment that equals or exceeds the sum of tax, penalty, and interest due thereon. Interest *does* continue to accrue on any difference not paid.

There is a major advantage to paying with a cash

bond. A bond must be returned at the taxpayer's request anytime before assessment of the tax, provided collection is not in jeopardy and no other tax liability exists. In contrast, a cash payment is not returnable at the taxpayer's request.

When an IRS official makes an error or fails to perform a ministerial act in a timely manner, the IRS may abate the interest attributable to the error or delays. Of course, the taxpayer must not be responsible for any significant aspect of the error or delay. Further, the delay or error must occur after the IRS has contacted you for the deficiency or payment. Use Form 843, Claim, to request the interest reduction.

You cannot be penalized for erroneous written advice furnished by the IRS. However, you must have requested the information in writing, provided accurate and adequate information to the IRS, and relied on the advice. Furthermore, you will have to prove that you received the advice in writing; advice received over the telephone, from a meeting with an IRS representative, or from IRS publications does not meet this criterion. It is a good idea to note the names of IRS employees from whom you receive advice.

18

STATUTE OF LIMITATIONS

If you find an error or omission on your return after it has been filed, you have time to file an amended return. The IRS also has a time period in which to make an examination—or further examination—of any return.

The term "statute of limitations" refers to the period after a tax return has been filed within which the government may seek additional taxes or the taxpayer may claim that an overpayment has occurred. Upon expiration of the period of limitations, the taxable period in question is considered closed. The slate is wiped clean for taxpayers; the government may keep the tax it collected for the period. The principle of limitations has an important place in U.S. tax law. Without it, many controversies would come up long after the tax year involved.

Generally, limitation periods begin on either the date the tax return is filed or the due date of the return (disregarding extensions), whichever is later. The period for filing a claim for refund or credit of an overpayment of tax is three years from the date of filing the return *or* two years from the date the tax was paid, whichever is later. If you do not file a tax return, any claim must be filed within two years from the time the tax was paid.

For example, if you file your 1990 tax return on January 31, 1991, your limitations period begins on the due date of the return: April 15, 1991. Accordingly, the period within which you may file a refund claim expires on April 15, 1994. The government has the same period to declare a return deficient. In other words, the IRS must impose the tax within three years of the date the return was filed or, if later, within three years of its due date. But say you didn't pay the tax until January 1, 1993. The statute is in effect for two years from this date—until January 1, 1995.

If a taxpayer omits more than 25 percent of gross income from the tax return, the period of limitation is six years. When no tax return is filed or the return is fraudulent, the statute of limitations does not apply.

In any tax dispute, you should be able to prove when you filed your return. A return sent by U.S. mail is considered delivered on the date of the postmark and not the date it is received by the IRS. You should get a receipt for your tax return from the post office. Use certified mail, return receipt requested, which can be used as evidence that you filed on time. If you file by electronic mail, you receive immediate confirmation that the IRS has received your tax return.

19

HOW THE IRS SELECTS TAX RETURNS FOR AUDIT

In any given year, your odds of being audited are slightly greater than one in a hundred.

The IRS uses several methods to select returns for audit:

1. Discriminant Function Program (see Key 21)
2. Document Matching Program
3. Targeted Items Program
4. Taxpayer Compliance Measurement Program
5. Tips from other taxpayers (see Key 22)
6. Investigating a business association with another person or entity who is audited
7. Targeting taxpayers who file amended returns.

The Document Matching Program is a computerized system used to match third-party information on items such as wages, interest, dividends, and certain deductions with the amounts reported by taxpayers. The IRS also uses third-party information to identify people who have received income but have not filed returns.

Each year, as many as one-fifth of the returns audited are picked under the IRS's Targeted Items Program. Some of the IRS's favorite targets are illegal tax protesters, narcotics traffickers, and people with tip income, tax shelters, casualty losses, Schedule C's, or home offices.

In recent years, the IRS has been closely monitoring the expense accounts of small businesses. The IRS is looking for abuses of travel and entertainment advances, research and development, long-term contracts, and property transfers. Advances to owners of small businesses must be used only for business-related activities; money not spent in this fashion must be returned within a reasonable period of time.

During 1990, the IRS began a campaign to audit 18,000 defined-benefit retirement plans covering one to five persons. Under this campaign, agents examine plans that allow participants to retire earlier than age 65 or that have an earnings rate of less than 8 percent. Those being targeted include individual professionals, small law firms, medical practices, consulting companies, and other small companies.

Under the Taxpayer Compliance Measurement Program (TCMP), the IRS chooses approximately 56,000 tax returns every three years at random from a sample based on taxpayers' social security numbers. If selected, you are an IRS guinea pig and must go through a nerve-wracking line-by-line scrutiny of your entire tax return. These audits are time-consuming and costly, because you must have records for *all* transactions and entries. The purpose of this program is to gather data to fine-tune the IRS's Discriminant Function Formula (see Key 21) and to evaluate the level of voluntary compliance. The most recent TCMP campaign, based on 1988 returns, was completed around May 31, 1991.

A business association with another person or entity who is audited may result in your being audited as well. A partner may be the cause, or the IRS may distrust your tax return preparer. In addition, the IRS audits a high percentage of amended returns—especially those claiming a refund—although they deny that filing an amended return will trigger an audit.

Other red flags that may increase the chances of being audited are claims for large refunds, late returns, and tax returns that do not match information returns or Social Security Administration reports. Taxpayers who are subject to the alternative minimum tax, who make valuable noncash charitable contributions, or who may be in collusion with another taxpayer seem to have a higher risk of being audited.

20

HOW THE IRS RECONSTRUCTS TAXPAYER INCOME

The IRS has several ways to reconstruct a taxpayer's income. The main ones are the net worth, cash expenditures, and bank deposit methods.

The *net worth method* is an indirect technique frequently used in both civil and criminal income tax cases. Suppose that someone you know bought a $1 million house last year, drives a very expensive car, wears custom-made clothing and precious gemstones, and boasts of being debt free. An IRS agent notes the new address (the ZIP code indicates an expensive neighborhood), yet the taxpayer reported a meager $15,000 of gross income. Where did this person get the money to live so well? If the IRS can show an increase in net worth, it will claim that the increase is taxable income. Perhaps the taxpayer can show otherwise—that the income was an inheritance, for example.

Determination of a person's net worth is done at the beginning and end of the period under investigation. The difference between the two amounts is the change in net worth. Adjustments are then made for nondeductible and nontaxable items.

To determine net worth, the IRS establishes a value for all of a taxpayer's assets, liabilities, and nondeductible expenses and the sources and amounts of nontaxable income. The IRS lists these values at cost (not market value) or at the taxpayer's basis for determining gain or loss if different from cost. The IRS may have to estimate the amount and value of a taxpayer's personal assets at the beginning of the year. Also, when using the net worth method for audit purposes, the IRS must use the accounting procedures used by the taxpayer.

The *cash expenditures method,* also called the *cash transactions method* and the *source and application of funds method,* is a commonly used indirect method of estimating taxable income. All known amounts of income are compared with all known expenditures. If your expenditures during a given period exceed reported income, without an explained source of funds, the difference represents unreported income.

For example, suppose you spent a lot of money last year but you don't have a big house or fancy car. Instead, you enjoy expensive restaurant meals, entertain with lavish parties, and send your children to expensive colleges. The IRS may find your true income indirectly, by adding up your expenditures. With some adjustments—such as money borrowed and savings spent—your income should equal your expenditures.

The cash expenditures approach is used when:
- a taxpayer has several assets and/or liabilities that did not change during the year;
- comparative balance sheets are available;
- there is little or no apparent net worth and most expenditures consist of nondeductible personal living expenses.

IRS agents use the cash expenditures approach to correct income in certain situations and to determine whether to perform a more detailed audit. If income appears correct, then a routine audit is in order. But if income appears understated, then a more detailed examination of the taxpayer's return may be indicated.

The *bank deposit method* is another indirect method the IRS uses to verify taxable income. Examiners obtain the taxpayer's bank account records and note all deposits. The burden of proof is on the taxpayer to explain why any deposit is not taxable. So, whenever you receive money, be sure to note its source in your records, especially if the receipt is nontaxable.

IRS agents apply the bank deposit method to both business and nonbusiness returns. It is mostly used when a taxpayer has numerous cash expenses or when there are a large number of unsorted bills, invoices, and receipts submitted upon audit.

21

DISCRIMINANT FUNCTION FORMULA

The Discriminant Function Formula (DIF) is a computer program used by the IRS to screen tax returns and select returns for audit. Selection criteria are a closely guarded secret within the Internal Revenue Service.

The IRS developed DIF to predict tax underpayments from information contained in previous tax returns and audit documents. DIF identifies instances of underreported income, unusually large deductions, and other items that indicate the need for an audit. The IRS divides tax returns into classes based on the amount and sources of income, and a different DIF is assigned to each class. A return with a high DIF score is selected (or "pulled") for manual screening. DIF is constantly being revised as the IRS collects new data about income and expenditure patterns.

DIF parameters are pegged not only to income classes, but also to geographic areas. Different regions of the country are assigned different DIFs based upon typical characteristics of tax returns. For example, a state income tax deduction could send up a red flag for a tax return from Texas, which has no individual state income tax. Certain taxpayers, especially the self-employed and people with high income, are likely to generate high DIF scores because the possibility of income distortion is great among these people.

Possible characteristics in the DIF formula include:

1. Tax shelters
2. Tip income occupation: waiter/waitress, hairstylist, bartender
3. Potential for significant change in tax liability
4. The comparative size of an item in relationship to the overall return
5. Large itemized deduction in relationship to income
6. Character of the items being examined
7. Possible fraud
8. Home office deductions
9. High travel and entertainment expense, and deducting 20 percent of business-related meal and entertainment expenses, which is no longer allowed
10. Schedule C, business income and expenses
11. Large tax refund
12. Multiple refunds to same address
13. Vacation homes
14. Personal exemptions claimed by noncustodial parent
15. Hobby losses from sideline businesses
16. Claiming a nondeductible expense (e.g., personal interest)
17. Avoidance of the self-employment tax on self-employment income reported on a Form 1099
18. Shifting of passive losses to active income
19. Luxury automobiles
20. Shifting of miscellaneous deductions (subject to 2 percent floor) to Schedule C

21. Early distributions from a pension account or an IRA
22. Large casualty loss
23. Uncollectible bad-debt write-off
24. Employee business expenses
25. Low reported income in expensive area (by ZIP code)
26. Low reported income with high interest expense

22

INFORMERS' PROGRAM

The IRS has a formal informers' program. Rewards, also called "fink fees," range from 1 to 10 percent of the taxes and penalties collected. In recent years, the IRS has received more than 10,000 tips annually.

From 1967 through 1989, approximately 134,000 tips were submitted. Only about 9 percent of all informers were paid; total payments to informers amounted to about $15 million. In 1989, there were approximately 12,000 tips, but the IRS paid only about 500 claims, with the average payment about $3,000.

We mention this program not to encourage you to become an informer but to encourage you to report your income honestly. You never know when an unhappy ex-spouse or former friend may decide you've been cheating long enough. Incidentally, whistle-blowers are themselves checked—the IRS is likely to audit returns of informers to be certain that these people owe no taxes and that they report the "fink fee."

The IRS also employs between 700 and 900 undercover informants. Some of them are accountants and other types of tax return preparers. Communications between clients and accountants are not confidential under federal law as attorney-client communications are.

23

TYPES OF AUDITS

Being audited is not a pleasant experience, but neither is it an accusation of wrongdoing. As defined by the IRS, an audit is an impartial review of a tax return to determine its accuracy and completeness. There are three main types of audits:

1. Correspondence
2. Office
3. Field

At the various IRS service centers, tax returns are reviewed for obvious errors such as overstated standard deductions, incorrect tax calculation, and incorrect filing status (improperly claiming to be a head of household, for example). The taxpayer receives a computer-printed letter proposing a correction in the tax. Administrative and judicial avenues of recourse are depicted in the chart on the following page. If a taxpayer's return is selected for examination and the return is relatively simple or a minor point is in question, a *correspondence audit* may occur. The IRS writes to the taxpayer to request information. Once the IRS is satisfied, the issue is settled.

A tax return may be selected for an *office audit.* In this case, the taxpayer is asked to present tax records and supporting information to the director's office at a prescribed date and time. A taxpayer has a number of rights during this process. Many office audits are begun and completed in a single session. If agreement is not reached with the examining officer, the taxpayer has the right to confer with an

Exhibit 2
Income Tax Appeal Procedure

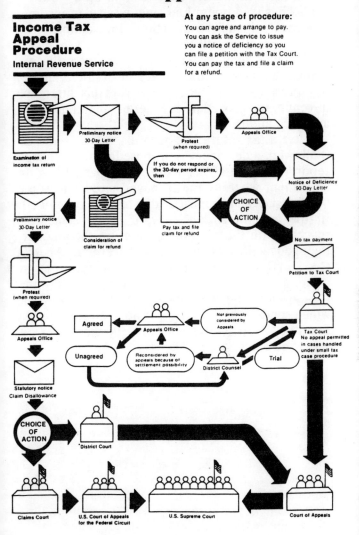

Income Tax Appeal Procedure
Internal Revenue Service

At any stage of procedure:
You can agree and arrange to pay.
You can ask the Service to issue you a notice of deficiency so you can file a petition with the Tax Court.
You can pay the tax and file a claim for a refund.

Examination of income tax return

Preliminary notice 30-Day Letter

Protest (when required)

Appeals Office

If you do not respond or the 30-day period expires, then

Notice of Deficiency 90-Day Letter

CHOICE OF ACTION

Preliminary notice 30-Day Letter

Consideration of claim for refund

Pay tax and file claim for refund

No tax payment

Petition to Tax Court

Protest (when required)

Appeals Office

Statutory notice Claim Disallowance

Agreed

Unagreed

Appeals Office

Not previously considered by Appeals

Reconsidered by appeals because of settlement possibility

District Counsel

Trial

Tax Court No appeal permitted in cases handled under small tax case procedure

CHOICE OF ACTION

*District Court

Claims Court

U.S. Court of Appeals for the Federal Circuit

U.S. Supreme Court

Court of Appeals

appeals officer to see if a settlement can be worked out. A written request will get a conference in an office audit case.

If a tax return is relatively complicated—if it includes business operations, many types of income, or intricate financial transactions, for example—the IRS examination will be conducted as a *field audit*. This means that the IRS agent conducts the examination at your office, place of business, home, or representative's office. Aside from this difference in venue, the procedure is generally the same as for an office audit.

After a tax return has been examined, a refund is allowed, a deficiency is proposed, or a no-change report or "partial" is issued. A "partial" is an agreement whereby the taxpayer accedes to some of the issues and proposed adjustments, but not all. In the case of a deficiency, if no agreement is reached with the examining agent on the amount, the agent writes what is called a Revenue Agent's Report (RAR). The agent submits the report to his or her group manager, who in turn submits it to the review staff. The case then goes to the 30-day unit, which sends a 30-day letter. If no protest is filed, a Statutory Notice of Deficiency (90-day letter) is sent. See Keys 31 and 32.

24

THE AUDIT PROCESS

Once a taxpayer submits a return to the IRS, it goes through an IRS computer that checks for mathematical accuracy and completeness. (See Exhibit 1, page 35.) The IRS uses a computerized program to match third-party information returns (e.g., W-2s, 1099s)—such as for wages, interest, dividends, and certain deductions—with the amounts reported on the tax returns. Computers also process this information to identify taxpayers who have received income but have not filed tax returns. When information returns do not agree with a filed tax return, the taxpayer is sent a letter that asks for an explanation of the discrepancy. In 1989, about 3.65 million of these letters were sent out.

Computers also check to see whether other items, such as deductions, interest, dividend income, and capital gains, fall within normal ranges. The Discriminant Function Formula (DIF) picks tax returns that are likely to contain errors, cheating, or understatement of taxes.

The audit procedure starts when you get a letter from the IRS informing you that your tax return is to be examined and specifying whether the examination is an office or field audit. Don't let the letter scare you. Just get prepared.

Two comments. First, never give original records to an agent or to the IRS. Instead, give copies. If you give original documentation, you run the risk of losing it. Second, if a "special agent" is conducting the audit, the IRS may suspect fraud, and you should obtain a lawyer immediately. Also, if you hear of an IRS agent checking with your bank or stockbroker or asking your neighbor questions about you, get a lawyer and take your records from your accountant or any other nonlawyer tax adviser. Communication with a nonlawyer is not considered privileged.

25

DEALING WITH THE AGENT OR AUDITOR

IRS personnel are human. Like you, they are under great stress; they must deal with rude taxpayers, arrogant tax practitioners, and an unyielding bureaucracy. Given this high-pressure environment, it is best to avoid acrimony in dealing with them. It is in your best interest to be courteous, respectful, cheerful, and cooperative.

During an audit interview, answer only the questions asked. You may save a lot of time—and anxiety—if you can get the auditor to state at the outset what he or she is looking for. Answer questions truthfully—but you need not tell everything. There is a fine line between providing enough information and providing too much. Think of the auditor as a factfinder, but don't suggest new areas of inquiry.

Allow the auditor to look at your documents and records only once. In a field audit, do not allow the auditor access to a copy machine or to take original documents away from your premises. Do make copies of documents that the auditor requests.

Do not complain about the tax system. IRS people have to pay taxes also, and they see a lot of people who are not paying their share. You should appear to be willing to pay the taxes you owe, but no more. Never appear to be a tax protester.

Keep in mind that an auditor is examining you and your lifestyle as well as your tax return. Therefore, your appearance should not call attention to itself. For example, it may be a good idea to forgo wearing your Rolex watch or a mink coat to the audit.

An auditor is developing information to reach informed judgments about your:

- financial history and standard of living;
- the nature of your employment, to determine relationship with other entities and the existence of expense allowance and the like; this could include bartering, the potentially taxable exchange of merchandise or services;
- money or property received that was determined to be tax-exempt and/or nontaxable income; and
- potential for moonlighting income.

Some auditors also develop the following information:

- the real and personal property owned, including bank account;
- any purchases, sales, transfers, contributions, or exchanges of personal assets during the period; and
- the correctness of exemptions and dependents claimed.

An auditor is trained to look for:

- possibilities of omitted income;
- sources of income;
- possibility of "bartering" or "swapping" techniques;
- the method used to determine dividend income, interest income, and other income items;
- income from interest on income tax refunds and savings accounts that may not appear on the tax return or taxpayer's records.

Auditors are trained to ask you probing questions in these matters. If you answer "no," but an auditor can prove otherwise, the IRS may try to penalize you for a false statement, which is called a Title 18 violation.

Your conduct and method of doing business may suggest to an auditor that you are filing improper returns. Auditors are instructed to be alert to the following actions:

- repeated delays on the part of the taxpayer in making and keeping appointments for the examination;
- uncooperative attitude—e.g., not complying with requests for records and not furnishing adequate explanations for discrepancies or questionable items;
- failure to keep proper books and records, especially if previously advised to do so;
- destroying books and records without a plausible explanation;
- making false, misleading, and inconsistent statements;
- submitting false documents or affidavits to substantiate items on the return;
- altering records;
- using cash instead of bank accounts;
- engaging in illegal activities;
- failing to deposit all receipts;
- quick agreement to adjustments and undue concern about immediate closing of the case.

In an office or field audit, you are instructed to bring specific records. Have those records organized in a logical fashion. If your records indicate a businesslike approach to recordkeeping, your audit may be brief. Summary sheets that are backed up by receipts bolster your chances of receiving a no-change audit report. An auditor who has to spend time sorting out your records is more likely to disallow the item in question and may even uncover new problems.

If you agree with the auditor's findings, he or she may prepare Form 1902E (Form 4549 if the auditor is a revenue agent), detailing your adjustments and your agreement. Form 870 may be presented for your signature (see Key 42). If you sign the Form 870, the IRS can assess the tax. If the issue remains unsettled, the IRS will send a 30-day letter, Preliminary Notice of Deficiency. It will probably include a Form 870 for your signature.

When there is disagreement on an issue, be pleasant but firm. Be prepared to take your issue to a higher authority. Administrative appeals are heard by supervisors and appeals officers. Judicial appeals may be taken to U.S. District Court, U.S. Tax Court, or U.S. Claims Court, followed by Circuit Courts of Appeal, and finally the Supreme Court.

26

TAXPAYERS' BILL OF RIGHTS

In 1988, Congress established the Taxpayers' Bill of Rights. It gives taxpayers the right to be informed of their rights, to record interviews, and to be represented at in-person interviews. The Taxpayers' Bill of Rights also stipulates that taxpayers can obtain the services of an ombudsman in certain situations (see Key 41), protect certain property from levies (see Key 34), and obtain relief in U.S. tax courts.

When the IRS contacts you about a tax issue, it must provide a written statement of your rights and its obligations during the audit, appeals, refund, and collection processes. IRS Publication #1, *Your Rights As a Taxpayer,* fulfills this information requirement. This brochure states that "as a taxpayer, you have the right to be treated fairly, professionally, promptly, and courteously by IRS employees." The IRS's stated goal is to protect your rights so that you will have confidence in the integrity, efficiency, and fairness of our tax system.

In addition, the IRS is bound by the Taxpayers' Bill of Rights to try to avoid sending multiple statements as a result of a single audit, proposed deficiency, or collection action. If you have been audited for the same items in either of the two previous years and no change in your tax liability has been proposed, you should contact the IRS to see if it will drop the repeat examination.

In most circumstances, the IRS cannot make you attend an examination at an IRS office other than the one closest to your home. Similarly, it cannot conduct an audit at a taxpayer's place of business if doing so necessitates closing the business. The IRS *can* go to a taxpayer's business to establish facts, such as inventory and asset verifications. In determining the time and place of an interview, the IRS is permitted to take into account the possibility of physical danger to an agent.

A taxpayer is permitted, after giving advance notice (at least ten days) to the IRS, to tape-record an in-person interview. (Be advised, however, that you may put the agent on the spot by recording the interview.) IRS employees also are authorized to record taxpayer interviews, provided the taxpayer receives prior notice of such recording (again, ten days or more). The taxpayer can get a copy of a transcript of the recording upon request and payment of the cost.

Before initial in-person audit interviews, the IRS must explain to you the audit process and taxpayers' rights. Similarly, before initial in-person collection interviews, the IRS must explain to you the collection process and taxpayers' rights. For this purpose, routine telephone conversations are not considered initial interviews. A written statement handed to you at an audit or collection interview or within a short time before the interview is sufficient. The explanation (whether written or oral) must state that you have the right to suspend the interview to consult with a representative.

You may be represented during an interview by an attorney, a certified public accountant, an enrolled agent, an enrolled actuary, or any other person permitted to represent a taxpayer before the IRS, except one who is debarred or suspended from practice before the IRS. A representative needs a properly completed power of attorney from you. See Key 27 or IRS Circular 230 for more information.

If, during an interview, you wish to consult with your representative, the interview must be suspended for this purpose. However, if this right is abused—by repeated suspensions of interviews to contact different representatives, for example—the IRS may issue a summons. See Key 38.

Even if you send a representative to an interview, the IRS may ask you to be present if your representative is responsible for unreasonable delay or hindrance. In such a case, the IRS may bypass your representative and require that you attend the interview.

27

POWER OF ATTORNEY

If you are audited, you may grant another party power of attorney (POA). This person is authorized to act in your behalf in any capacity except receiving refund checks and signing tax returns.

A taxpayer can grant a power of attorney by using IRS Form 2848 or Form 2848D. The latter gives less authority to the designated person, so Form 2848D should be used whenever possible. A power of attorney may be granted without using Form 2848, but all information that would be provided on the IRS form must be provided. An unenrolled representative who does not file the form may be prohibited from receiving or inspecting certain tax information.

To be considered valid, a power of attorney must contain certain information about you. Your name, identification number, and address must be specified. If a joint return is being filed and both spouses are naming the same representative, the same information must be provided for the spouse. Your representative's name, Central Authorization File (CAF) number (if already assigned), address, and telephone number must be designated. The IRS assigns the CAF number after your representative files a Form 2848 or Form 2848D with an IRS office.

Other required information is the type of tax, the tax form number, and the year or period for which the power of attorney is granted. Also, the destination of written communications from the IRS should be specified. You (and your spouse if you are filing a joint return) should sign the POA form. Finally, you should get it notarized if the representative is not a CPA, attorney, or enrolled agent.

Your representative should file the POA form with each IRS office in which he or she serves you. A power of attorney may be changed by specifying the new authorization or representative on a new Form 2848 or 2848D. To revoke a power of attorney, you must prepare a new one or send a signed statement to each IRS office in which powers of attorney have been filed.

The law requires all persons to keep tax returns and tax information confidential. A violation is a felony offense, punishable by a fine of up to $5,000 and/or five years in prison. POAs can provide practitioners access to specific tax returns and account information. This arrangement safeguards information that taxpayers provide to the IRS.

28

CIVIL PENALTIES

The IRS has ways of encouraging taxpayers to discharge their tax obligations. One way is through civil penalties. There are almost 150 penalties in the tax code whose purpose is to curtail unethical and irresponsible conduct.

The civil penalty for *failing to file* a required tax return is 5 percent of the net amount of tax owed as of the due date each month, or fraction of a month, that the tax return is not filed, up to a maximum of 25 percent. The penalty for fraudulent failure to file a return is 15 percent per month, to a maximum of 75 percent. The IRS has the burden of proof on the fraud element of the penalty.

The Supreme Court has ruled that any minimally competent person should be able to ascertain the due date of a tax return and see that the return is filed. Thus, reliance on a tax adviser can be used as a defense for failure to file only when a taxpayer has provided full information to a competent tax adviser *and* the adviser determined that no tax return was due.

An accuracy-related penalty of 20 percent is assessed on any *underpayment of tax* that is attributable to negligence (not to the entire underpayment of tax). Negligence encompasses any careless, reckless, or intentional disregard of rules or regulations, and any failure to make a reasonable attempt to comply with the Internal Revenue Code.

Reliance on a tax adviser may be considered reasonable cause for purposes of the negligence penalty if you have given all the relevant information to an adviser who could be considered competent. Also, a taxpayer can negate the negligence penalty under a *reasonable cause and good faith* exception. The taxpayer completes a disclosure of the specific item on the tax return and clearly indicates the disclosure on the top of the first page of the tax return by writing: "Disclosure made under Section 6621." Reference the page or line number containing the disclosure. As an alternative, a taxpayer may use Form 8275 for disclosure. However, disclosure may flag a tax return for audit.

A 20 percent civil penalty is assessed for any *substantial understatement of income tax*. For individuals, a substantial understatement is the greater of 10 percent of the tax or $5,000. The amount of any understatement is reduced where the understatement is attributable to either an item for which there is substantial authority, or an item that was adequately disclosed on the return or a statement attached to the return.

"Substantial authority" refers to the Internal Revenue Code, court decisions, regulations, revenue rulings, proposed regulations, the Blue Book, IRS notices and announcements, technical advice memoranda, and letter rulings (published after 1984). The opinions of tax professionals and conclusions reached in books, magazines, and legal periodicals rendered are not considered substantial authority.

A 20 percent penalty is assessed for *valuation errors*. A substantial valuation overstatement exists if the value or adjusted basis of any property claimed on a tax return is 200 percent or more of the correct value or adjusted basis. This penalty is applied only if the amount of the underpayment exceeds $5,000 ($10,000 for corporations). The 20 percent rate is doubled if the value or adjusted basis claimed is 400 percent or more of the correct value or adjusted basis.

A 20 percent penalty is assessed for *substantial overstatement of pension liabilities* and for *substantial estate or gift tax valuation understatement*. The IRS may waive any part of the substantial understatement penalty if the taxpayer shows reasonable cause and good faith. Reliance on an information return, professional advice, or other sources may constitute reasonable cause and good faith.

If the IRS can prove fraud (see Key 29), it will most likely assess a 75 percent penalty. The 20 percent accuracy penalty does not apply to any portion of an understatement on which the fraud penalty is imposed. Once the IRS establishes that any part of the underpayment is due to fraud, the entire underpayment is treated as due to fraud unless the taxpayer can prove otherwise. Of course, the IRS initially has the burden of proof of establishing fraud.

Some penalties are designed to encourage taxpayers to file correct information returns and make required time deposits. The amount of the penalty varies with the length of time taken to correct the failure. Taxpayers who operate a business must be aware of these penalties and correct such failures as soon as possible.

A chart of some of the infractions and penalties follows:

Failure to file	*5 percent for each month or fraction, up to 25 percent*
Failure to pay	*0.5 percent of the tax not paid each month, up to a maximum of 25 percent. Monthly rate increases to 1 percent after issuance of Final Notice.*

(Continued on next page)

Frivolous return	*$500*
Negligence	*20 percent of underpayment attributable to negligence.*
Substantial understatement civil penalty	*20 percent*
Misevaluations	
* 200 percent or more overstatement*	*20 percent*
* 400 percent or more*	*40 percent*
Civil fraud	*75 percent*

29

FRAUD

Fraud is sometimes discovered in the course of an audit. Fraud is intentional deception to induce another to part with property or surrender some legal right. More simply, it is obtaining something of value from another party through deceit. Fraud may involve falsifying documents, tax returns, or statements. It includes attempted tax evasion; conspiracy to defraud; aiding, abetting, or counseling fraud; and willful failure to file income, estate, gift, and excise tax returns.

Civil fraud cases are remedial actions by the government to assess the correct tax and to impose civil penalties. Criminal fraud cases are actions with penalties of fines and/or imprisonment. Civil penalties are assessed and collected as part of the tax. Criminal penalties are intended to punish the taxpayer for wrongdoing and serve as a deterrent to other taxpayers. One offense may result in both civil and criminal penalties. For example, an accountant or bookkeeper may be charged with evading a client's or employer's taxes when helping to prepare false returns.

The three-year statute of limitations does not apply in civil fraud cases; tax and penalties may be assessed at any time. However, the statute of limitations for prosecution purposes (usually six years) runs from the time the offense was committed (usually considered to be the due date of the return). A criminal prosecution is not needed to assess the civil fraud penalty.

A major difference between civil and criminal fraud cases involves the degree of proof required. In criminal cases, the government must present evidence sufficient to prove guilt beyond a reasonable doubt. A lesser degree of proof is required in civil fraud cases. Evidence that is not sufficient to prove criminal fraud may be sufficient to prove civil fraud.

In order to establish fraud, the IRS must prove two basic facts:

1. Understatement of tax liability. A tax examiner must show that certain items were not completely or accurately reflected on the return, and that this resulted in an understatement of income (e.g., failure to report interest income or improper deduction of personal living expenses). The IRS may use indirect measures to prove the inaccuracy of a return. These measures include the net worth, source and application of funds, and bank deposit methods of reconstructing income. See Key 20.

2. Intent to avoid tax. The fact that income was understated does not prove that it was done intentionally. Failure to report the correct income may be due to mistake, inadvertence, reliance on professional advice, honest difference of opinion, negligence, or carelessness, none of which constitutes deliberate intent to defraud.

Intentional tax evasion occurs when a taxpayer knows that the misrepresentation of tax liability is false. Intent is a mental process, a state of mind. It is necessary to judge a taxpayer's intent by action. A person's words and actions are assumed to be the natural consequences of the person's intention.

In most taxpayer-IRS disputes, the burden of proof is on the taxpayer to overcome the presumption that the IRS determination is correct. *However, in a fraud case, the burden is on the IRS to prove that the taxpayer intended to evade the tax.* The degree of proof required in civil cases is the preponderance of evidence, except where fraud is alleged. In civil fraud cases, the IRS must produce "clear and convincing evidence," and it is necessary to prove only that *some part* of the deficiency was due to fraud.

30

PREPARER PENALTIES

Tax return preparers are also subject to a number of penalties and levies. As a rule, these are not covered by the preparer's malpractice insurance policy, and they are nondeductible for tax purposes. Furthermore, they may prompt the IRS to review all of the tax returns of the preparer's clients.

Failure of a preparer to furnish a copy of a return to a taxpayer, to sign the return, or to furnish an identification number carries a $50 penalty per return, up to a maximum of $25,000 per calendar year for each type of infraction. Failure to file a correct information return also carries a $50 penalty. Willful attempts to understate income and reckless or intentional disregard of IRS rules and regulations carry a $1,000 penalty. A preparer who has taken an "unrealistic position" may receive a $250 penalty. The IRS defines a "realistic" position as one that a person knowledgeable in tax law, after reasonable and well-informed analysis, would conclude has a one in three, or greater, likelihood of being sustained.

A return preparer can protect both the preparer and the taxpayer by adequately disclosing nonfrivolous positions. See Key 28 for a discussion of adequate disclosures.

The U.S. Tax Court may impose a penalty of up to $25,000 if it can show that a case has been brought as a delaying tactic, is frivolous, or was begun without pursuing administrative remedies (see Key 42). The IRS has not defined its use of the term *frivolous*. But the American Institute of Certified Public Accountants defines a frivolous position as one that is knowingly advanced in bad faith and is patently improper.

The penalty for directly or indirectly promoting abusive tax shelters is the smaller of $1,000 or 100 percent of gross income derived or to be derived from the activity.

A return preparer who knowingly or recklessly discloses or uses tax return information is guilty of a misdemeanor punishable by imprisonment and a criminal fine. The preparer may also receive a civil penalty of $250 for each offense, up to a maximum of $10,000 per calendar year. There is no penalty if the act was done under a court order or by a provision of the Internal Revenue Code.

31

POST-AUDIT RESPONSE

After an office audit, the IRS sends a "15-day letter" giving you an opportunity to submit additional evidence or information. Shortly afterward, you are mailed a "30-day letter" with a copy of the audit report and Form 870. This letter notifies you that within the next thirty days you have two options: (1) submit a written protest (if the proposed deficiency is more than $2,500) and ask for a conference with an appeals officer, or (2) sign a waiver agreeing to the proposed deficiency. Another option, available when the tax deficiency is between $2,500 and $10,000, is to submit a written statement (not in protest form) of the disputed issues. No written statement is required if the deficiency is less than $2,500.

If you don't respond to the 30-day letter, an official notice of the proposed assessment will be sent. This is a "Statutory Notice of Deficiency," sometimes called a "90-day letter."

At both the revenue agent and the Appeals Office level, if you agree to a proposed deficiency, you will be asked to sign a waiver using a form from the IRS's 870 series. Form 870A is used in prerefund situations, mostly by the Office of International Operations; 870C is for corporations; 870E is for exempt organizations; and 870I is for fiduciaries. Each of these forms bears a variation of the title "Waiver of Restrictions on Assessment and Collection of Deficiency in Tax and Acceptance of Over-assessments.''

Once you sign one of these forms, you waive your rights to a ''90-day letter'' and your right to appeal the matter to the U.S. Tax Court. Interest on any sum you owe the IRS stops accruing within thirty days after you sign Form 870. Both parties are considered in agreement, and the matter is closed—at least for the time being.

Unless you submit your payment along with the waiver, the IRS ordinarily sends you a bill for the amount of the proposed deficiency plus interest, to be paid within ten days. Even if a taxpayer signs Form 870 and the government accepts it, in most circumstances neither party is prohibited from taking further action. The taxpayer can still file a claim for refund, and the IRS can assess an additional deficiency. The only type of binding agreement at the administrative level is a *closing agreement* (Form 906). These agreements are often used at the Appeals Office level, especially when there are several matters in dispute, possibly involving more than one year. Use of Form 906 at the examination level is rare.

Ordinarily, however, the IRS closes its files on a tax return after receipt of Form 870 and payment of the deficiency.

32

THE 90-DAY LETTER

In unsettled tax matters, the IRS sends you, by registered or certified mail, a notice of the proposed assessment of a deficiency. The official name of this document is "Statutory Notice of Deficiency," but it is commonly referred to as a "90-day letter." The document gives you a period of ninety days (150 days if you are outside the country) to settle the matter or to file a petition with the U.S. Tax Court.

Your choices include the following:

1. Pay the tax.
2. Contact the nearest IRS Problem Resolution Office.
3. Seek a further settlement with the Appeals Office. Your case will be assigned there after your petition is filed.
4. Pay the tax and file suit for a refund in the district court or in the United States Claims Court.
5. File a petition in the U.S. Tax Court.
6. Use the Small Claims Division of the Tax Court for tax deficiencies that are under $10,000.
7. When responding to a 90-day letter, use certified or registered mail, return receipt requested, and be sure the postal clerk properly dates the materials. (There are no extensions to this ninety-day deadline, so be sure to re-

spond within that period. One taxpayer mailed a petition for Tax Court review of a proposed deficiency on the last day of the ninety-day filing period. The envelope was properly addressed, but it bore no postmark. It was not received by the IRS until the ninety-third day. "Tough luck," said the Tax Court. The petition was denied.)

33

IRS COLLECTION PROCESS

If you don't respond to a Statutory Notice of Deficiency (90-day letter), the IRS will assess the deficiency. *Assessment* is the act of officially recording the amount owed by the taxpayer.

Once an assessment officer signs an assessment summary record, the collection process begins. The IRS's current policy is to send four "Notice and Demand" forms (Forms 501, 502, 503, and 504), each with more threatening language than the previous one, at intervals of four to five weeks. If the taxpayer does not pay the deficiency within ten days of receipt of a "Final Notice" (Form 504), the IRS can begin collection enforcement procedures. Enforcement may begin earlier if delay is thought to impair collectibility—for example, in a jeopardy assessment.

If a tax account remains delinquent after the four notices, the IRS will issue a Notice of Levy against the taxpayer's assets. This notice authorizes the IRS to seize income and assets to satisfy the account. If there are no known sources of income or the IRS does not receive sufficient funds, the account will be assigned to a collection officer or to the automated collection system (ACS).

ACS is a computer that automatically dials a delinquent taxpayer's home or business telephone number. When the taxpayer answers, an IRS representative comes on the line to discuss the collection. Cases involving large sums of money might be assigned directly to a revenue officer, who determines the taxpayer's ability to pay and determines whether seizable assets exist.

Uncollectible accounts do occur because of bankruptcy, death, or hardship. Though bankruptcy discharges some debts, the IRS usually does not forgive the tax debt. Tax liens remain on file, and any tax overpayments are used to offset delinquent tax liability.

There is, however, a statute of limitations (generally six years) on the collection of tax after assessment (see Key 18).

34

LIENS AND LEVIES

The IRS's levy authority is far-reaching. The IRS has the power to collect taxes by distraint or seizure of assets, even assets held by other parties. A levy permits continuous attachment of the nonexempt portion of your wages and allows the seizure and sale of your assets. However, a levy can claim property held by the taxpayer and third parties only at the time of the levy itself.

The IRS must notify you by certified or registered mail thirty days before imposing a levy on your property. The notice must be a brief statement in simple, nontechnical terms. This notice and waiting-period requirements do not apply if the IRS believes that tax collection is in jeopardy. Unless the collection of tax is in jeopardy, the IRS cannot place a levy on your property on a day when you must attend a collection interview.

Certain property is exempt from levy:

1. Up to $1,650 of fuel, provisions, furniture, and personal household effects.
2. Up to $1,100 of books, tools, machinery, and equipment necessary for the trade, business, or profession of the taxpayer.
3. Unemployment and job-training benefits, workers' compensation, welfare, certain disability payments, and certain pension benefits.
4. The income you need to pay court-ordered child support.
5. Mail.
6. An amount of weekly income equal to your

standard deduction and personal exemptions, divided by 52.

7. Your primary residence (with some exceptions).

8. Property that is worth less than it would cost to levy and sell it.

If your bank account is levied, your bank is legally obligated to hold the account up to the amount of the levy for twenty-one days. This period provides time to resolve your tax bill before the bank turns over the funds to the IRS.

The amount of weekly wages exempt from IRS levy is your standard deduction and allowable personal exemptions, divided by 52. If you do not supply the IRS with information sufficient to make this calculation, the amount of wages exempt is the standard deduction for a married individual filing separately plus one personal exemption, divided by 52.

Under most circumstances, the IRS can seize your property without a court order. However, you don't have to allow access to your private premises—such as your home or the nonpublic areas of your business—to anyone who doesn't have a search warrant.

As of June 30, 1989, a taxpayer's principal residence is exempt from levy unless an IRS district director or assistant director approves the levy in writing or collection of the tax is deemed to be in jeopardy.

35

RELEASE OF LIENS AND LEVIES

Under federal law, the IRS must release a levy on property if:

1. The liability for which the levy was made is satisfied.
2. The IRS determines that release will help collect the liability.
3. An approved installment-payment agreement has been signed (see Key 40).
4. The IRS has determined that the levy is creating an economic hardship for the taxpayer.
5. The fair market value of the property exceeds the liability, and partial release would not hinder collection of the tax and other amounts owed to the IRS.
6. The IRS's status as a secured creditor will not be jeopardized.

The release of a levy does not prevent a subsequent levy on the same property. During the collection process, you can discuss your case with a supervisor if you do not agree with the collection officer.

If the IRS seizes your property, you can request that it be sold within a certain period of time (sixty days or more). The IRS must comply with your request unless it is not in the best interests of the government. Since June 30, 1988, IRS levies upon tangible personal property needed in the taxpayer's trade or business must provide for an accelerated appeals process to determine whether the levy should be released.

There is a procedure to obtain review of a notice of lien in the public record and an opportunity to release the lien. This procedure is designed to correct erroneous filings, not to challenge the tax deficiency that caused the lien. If the IRS determines that filing a notice of lien was erroneous (perhaps the owed tax was paid earlier or the lien violated the restrictions on assessment), the IRS must issue (within fourteen days) a release-of-lien certificate, including a statement that the filing was erroneous. This ensures that the public record contains a statement that the notice of the lien was not the taxpayer's fault. A certificate of release may help repair the damage to the taxpayer's credit and other financial records.

You may bring suit in a federal district court if an IRS agent knowingly or negligently fails to release a lien. You may recover up to the greater of IRS-caused direct economic damages to you or $100 per day (up to $1,000) for each day the lien remains unreleased, beginning ten days after the IRS is notified.

36

BANKRUPTCY AND UNPAID TAXES

As a rule, there is no discharge of taxes for an individual taxpayer who files a bankruptcy petition. This includes prepetition taxes and taxes for which no return—or a late or fraudulent return—was filed. However, taxes that were due three years or more before the bankruptcy petition is filed may be discharged.

Prepetition taxes include:

- Income taxes for returns that were due up to three years before bankruptcy.
- Income taxes assessed up to 240 days before bankruptcy.
- Income taxes that were not assessed but were assessable after the bankruptcy petition was filed.
- Withholding taxes for which the debtor is liable.
- Employment taxes on the first $2,000 of wages, salaries, and commissions earned by each employee of the debtor due within ninety days before filing bankruptcy or winding up a business; and employment taxes due up to three years before filing bankruptcy.
- Excise taxes for which a tax return was due up to three years before bankruptcy.
- Taxes in the course of the debtor's business or financial affairs in an involuntary bankruptcy, after filing in bankruptcy but before a trustee is appointed or the order for relief is given.

When an individual files for bankruptcy under Chapter 7 (liquidation) or 11 (reorganization) of the Bankruptcy Code, an "estate" is created. This estate is a taxable entity holding the property of the bankrupt debtor.

The bankruptcy estate is managed by a trustee. An individual who has filed for bankruptcy is given a fresh start—wages earned and property bought cannot be garnished. By contrast, an estate is not created by an individual who files a Chapter 13 bankruptcy (wage-earner's plan), or when a corporation or partnership files for bankruptcy.

IRS publication 908, *Bankruptcy and Other Debt Cancellation,* offers more detail on this subject.

37

SAFE-DEPOSIT BOXES

You can't use a safe-deposit box to prevent the IRS from garnishing your assets, because the box can be opened without your consent. Most safe-deposit boxes have two keys: a master key the bank or trust company holds, and a key held by the renter.

A bank or trust company will not open a safe-deposit box without the consent of the renter unless directed to do so by a court order. The IRS can prevent you from having access to the box, or it can obtain a court order directing that the box be opened—by force if necessary.

Since assets other than cash may be in the safe-deposit box, the IRS should file a notice of lien before seizure. The IRS serves a notice of levy, Form 668A, with a copy of the notice of lien attached, on an officer of the bank or trust company that owns the box and requests that the contents of the box be surrendered.

The bank may claim that it does not have the key to the safe-deposit box or does not have the authority to open it. It may also suggest to the IRS agent that your consent be secured, or that a court order be obtained to open the box. If so, the IRS will not insist that the box be opened. Instead, the box is sealed with a seizure notice, the Seal for Securing Safety Deposit Boxes. Once this seal is affixed, the box cannot legally be opened except in the presence of a revenue officer.

Eventually, the rental period of the safe-deposit box will expire. When that happens, a bank or trust company may have the right to open the box and seize its contents.

In some cases, this procedure is not satisfactory to the IRS. For instance, the statute of limitations may be about to expire, the taxpayer may be incommunicado, or the taxpayer or bank may deny access to the safe-deposit box. Under these circumstances, a summons will be served on the taxpayer-boxholder in an attempt to secure information on the contents of the box and to gain access. If this action proves fruitless, the IRS can obtain a writ of entry or bring suit to have the box opened.

38

SUMMONSES

Tax law gives the IRS the power to subpoena a taxpayer and witnesses for testimony and force them to produce records for examination. A summons identifies the taxpayer under investigation, the district and time periods involved in the investigation, and the documents being sought.

The IRS issues summonses to taxpayers or third parties who refuse to cooperate with a request for information. Probable cause is not necessary; the IRS can enforce its summons power when testimony or materials are needed to obtain a tax return, determine tax liability, or provide information about tax law violations.

Only documents specifically requested in a summons should be turned over to the IRS. You should maintain detailed records and photocopies of all documents you place in the IRS's hands. Once documents have been summonsed, you cannot destroy them without the risk of criminal prosecution.

The IRS's summons power is of particular importance to accountants and attorneys. In its *Arthur Young* v. *Tiffany Fine Arts* decision, the Supreme Court decreed that the IRS's summons power can force an accountant to turn over certain work-related documents. This extension of power allows the IRS to require third-party recordkeepers to turn over documents relating to their tax-planning strategies. By doing so, tax practitioners are exposing their analysis of a taxpayer's position. Consequently, accountants and attorneys should not produce unnecessary documents and should periodically destroy outdated and irrelevant materials.

39

TAXPAYER
APPLICATION FOR
HARDSHIP RELIEF

You, your representative, or any IRS employee may file Form 911, Application For a Taxpayer Assistance Order to Relieve Hardship (ATAO). You can obtain Form 911 by calling 1-800-424-1040. You should mail it back by certified, registered, or express mail.

Form 911, so numbered to suggest the near-universal emergency phone number, is used to request a review of a case in which an enforcement action taken has caused or would cause a hardship. There should be a current or imminent hardship, either through IRS action (e.g., enforcement actions) or lack of action (e.g., delayed refunds) that the IRS employee contacted cannot or will not rectify.

The IRS must immediately prepare Form 911 and forward it to the PRP office (see Key 41) whenever:
• there is an existing or impending hardship on the taxpayer; and,
• the IRS employee dealing with the problem cannot or will not relieve the hardship immediately.

Appropriate appeal procedures should be used before resorting to the ATAO. IRS employees are instructed to invoke the "stop and review" feature of an ATAO whenever possible.

The IRS recognizes a number of taxpayer hardships, including emotional stress, the threat of a poor credit rating, imminent bankruptcy, failure to meet payroll, gross disservice to the taxpayer, pending eviction, and possible loss of job. Hardship is determined on a case-by-case basis.

Imminent hardships include actions that are occurring (e.g., the bank has received a levy but has not acted on it yet). They also include ones that have just occurred (e.g., property has been seized but not sold) or are about to occur (e.g., a refund is needed immediately for a medical emergency).

If you are experiencing a hardship in paying a tax bill but are able to make an installment agreement (see Key 40), an ATAO should not be needed. For example, if there is an impending enforcement action but you are able to resolve the problem immediately with the IRS, you need not file an ATAO.

Sometimes an ATAO is warranted because IRS enforcement actions are inappropriate. For example, suppose you provide information to explain an issue and the IRS does not consider the response. Instead, it issues a Notice of Deficiency (90-day letter). You write to the service center again but receive no response. With ten days remaining on the 90-day letter, you file a Form 911. You state that you have provided the information requested, but it has not been considered and you cannot afford the cost of filing a petition to the Tax Court and professional fees.

An ATAO may not be used to suspend the 90-day period, but it may be used to extend the period for assessment. This process allows the IRS to rescind the Notice of Deficiency until the account is reviewed and your information is considered.

40

INSTALLMENT AGREEMENTS

Suppose you are simply unable to pay the taxes that you owe. You and the IRS can enter into a written installment-payment agreement. It is probably better to borrow the money elsewhere, but an installment agreement is a reasonable alternative. The interest rate may be lower than that on many types of personal loans (although, in most cases, the Failure to Pay Penalty assessed by the IRS makes this option more costly). Keep in mind, however, that the IRS doesn't want to be a lender—and it has great authority to attach your bank accounts, stocks, or bonds if a satisfactory payment arrangement cannot be reached.

An installment agreement remains in effect for its term unless you (1) provided inaccurate or incomplete information, (2) miss a payment, (3) fail to pay any other tax liability when due, (4) fail to respond to any reasonable request to supply updated financial information, or (5) the IRS determines that the collection of any tax you agreed to pay is in jeopardy.

Installment agreements are negotiated directly with the IRS. Collection Division officers interview candidates for these agreements to determine ability to pay the overdue taxes. The following assets and sources of funds are examined in making this determination:

- Cash
- Marketable securities
- Cash surrender value of life insurance policies
- Equity on unencumbered assets and remaining equity on encumbered assets
- Available lines of credit

After these sources have been exhausted, the IRS applies the taxpayer's expected salary to the tax deficiency, allowing for expenses in the following areas:

- Child care
- Medical care
- Rent, food, and home maintenance
- Necessary clothing and transportation
- Taxes
- Court-ordered payment obligations
- Car payments
- Accrued credit card balances that cannot be deferred
- Religious or educational purposes

The IRS may modify or terminate an installment-payment agreement if it determines that your financial condition has significantly changed. This action may be taken only if the IRS notifies you at least thirty days before acting and gives the reason.

The Taxpayers' Bill of Rights guarantees that if you provide complete and accurate information to the IRS and satisfy all tax liabilities when due, including installment payments, the installment agreement cannot be revoked.

41

PROBLEM RESOLUTION PROGRAM

If you have a tax problem that cannot be resolved through normal channels, you may wish to consult a problem resolution officer (PRO). Each IRS district, service center, and regional office has a problem resolution program, directed by a PRO who serves as a taxpayer ombudsman. PROs handle taxpayers' complaints and, by identifying the causes of complaints, seek to prevent similar problems from occurring in the future. They are supposed to represent the interests and concerns of taxpayers who have become entangled in the IRS system.

PROs may intervene if IRS action or inaction would cause a taxpayer hardship. In such cases, PROs can call for a review of a case to determine if IRS action is correct and appropriate. They also can take steps to speed up an action, such as expediting a refund or releasing a lien.

PROs also have the authority to approve replacement checks for certain lost or stolen refunds, substantiate credits to taxpayers' accounts when the taxpayer can prove payment but the IRS cannot locate the payment, and reverse certain penalties if taxpayers have a reasonable cause.

A taxpayer ombudsman has authority to issue a taxpayer assistance order (TAO) if he or she determines that a taxpayer is suffering or about to suffer a hardship resulting from an IRS action. The ombudsman may take action whether or not a taxpayer has filed an application requesting relief. TAOs call for a remedial action, such as releasing taxpayer property from seizure. A TAO is binding on the IRS unless it is modified or rescinded by the ombudsman or another IRS employee.

The normal statute of limitations is suspended starting when a taxpayer files an application for a TAO and ending when the ombudsman decides on the application. The statute of limitations is not suspended when an ombudsman issues an order that is not in response to an application for relief.

42

ADMINISTRATIVE
APPEAL PROCESS

If you agree with the findings in a tax examiner's report, you will be asked to sign Form 870. This stops interest from accruing thirty days after it is filed (unless the tax has not been assessed). The form lists the tax deficiency and penalties and allows the IRS to begin collection procedures. The agreement with the agent is not binding on the IRS *or* the taxpayer. You can still file a claim for a refund (after paying the tax). If the IRS disallows your claim, you may pursue refund litigation in a district court or in Claims Court.

If you disagree with the findings—or have any problem at all with the examiner—a meeting with the examiner's supervisor to discuss the findings may prove productive. If not, you may appeal your case within the IRS. Most disagreements can be settled in these appeals, which avoid expensive and time-consuming court trials. However, an appeal for conference is not granted if the taxpayer's grounds for disagreement are beyond the scope of the internal revenue laws—for example, moral, religious, or political reasons.

Appeals within the IRS are handled by the Office of Regional Director of Appeals. Address your request for a conference to your district director in accordance with any instructions you have received. The district director will forward your request to the Appeals Office, which will schedule the conference. Appeals officers are located in most major cities. In 1989, appeals closed about 89,000 cases, of which 90 percent were agreed to by the taxpayer.

Along with your request for a conference, you may need to file a written protest with the district director. A brief written statement is acceptable when a field audit results in a proposed change between $2,500 and $10,000. No written statement is needed when the proposed increase or decrease in tax, or claimed refund, does not exceed $2,500 for any of the tax periods involved.

If a written protest or brief statement is required, mail it within the prescribed period granted in the letter you received, with the report of examination, and include:

1. A statement that you want to appeal the findings of the examiner to the Appeals Office.
2. Your name and address.
3. The date and symbols from the letter you received with the proposed adjustments and findings you are protesting.
4. The tax periods or years involved.
5. An itemized schedule of the adjustments with which you disagree.
6. A statement of facts supporting your position on any contested issue.
7. A statement outlining the law or other authority on which you rely.

The statement of facts, under 6 above, must be declared true under penalties of perjury. To do this, add the following signed declaration:

Under penalties of perjury, I declare that the facts presented in this protest, which are set out in the accompanying statement of facts, schedules, and other attached statements, are to the best of my knowledge and belief true, correct, and complete.

If your representative sends the protest for you, he or she may substitute a declaration stating:
- that he or she prepared the protest and accompanying documents; and
- whether he or she knows personally that statement of facts in the protest and accompanying documents are true and correct.

You may represent yourself before Appeals, or be represented by an attorney, a certified public accountant, or an enrolled agent. If your representative appears without you, he or she must file a power of attorney (see Key 27) or a tax information authorization before receiving or inspecting confidential information.

You may also bring witnesses to support your position. The proceedings are informal, and the appeals officer can raise a new issue and can propose a new theory to support the IRS agent.

Revenue agents must follow regulations, revenue rulings, and other IRS releases. There are many areas of uncertainty. An appeals officer will consider the hazards and, to a much lesser extent, the expenses of resolving an issue through litigation. The officer may decide to split or trade issues with the taxpayer in order to settle a dispute.

If the IRS agent reaches a decision that you accept, the matter is ended. Otherwise, you may concede or pursue further remedies. If you accept the IRS decision, you will be asked to sign Form 870AD, a waiver that is similar to others of the Form 870 series, but with important differences:

1. Form 870 is effective with the signature of the taxpayer, though it does not bar the taxpayer from later filing a claim for refund (within the period of limitations), nor does it bar the IRS from future assertion of a deficiency.

2. Form 870AD requires the acceptance and signature of a properly authorized representative of the IRS. It says that it bars the taxpayer from later filing a claim for refund, although that point is not settled in law.

3. The printed terms of Form 870AD are frequently modified by insertions or changes that, if sponsored by the IRS, the taxpayer should review carefully lest valuable rights be signed away.

43

JUDICIAL REMEDIES

If you are not satisfied after your appeal to the Appeals Office, you need not sign Form 870AD. Instead, you may go to one of the trial courts to seek redress. There are three courts of original jurisdiction in the United States: Tax Court, District Court, and Claims Court. Above them are the appellate courts, including the courts of appeal of the various circuits and the Supreme Court. These courts have no connection with the IRS. (See Exhibit 2: Income Tax Appeal Procedure.) There is a small claims division within the Tax Court, as described in Key 44.

The U.S. Tax Court has nineteen judges, appointed by the President with the advice and consent of the Senate. The term of office is fifteen years. The judges sometimes come from the ranks of high officials of the IRS, and they are usually well acquainted with tax matters. Further, the chief judge may appoint a commissioner to hear testimony, make findings, and recommend the type of decision to be rendered in any case.

The Tax Court's jurisdiction covers all fifty states. From it, appeals go to the thirteen U.S. Circuit courts of appeal. An appeal must be made to the circuit court that covers the area where the taxpayer lives.

Before deciding which course to pursue, pause for serious thought and consult with your representative. The jurisdiction of the Tax Court is limited to cases involving proposed deficiencies in a tax not yet paid. If you pay the proposed deficiency and file a claim for refund that is denied or not acted upon within six months, you can sue for a refund either in a federal district court or in the Claims Court in Washington, D.C. A taxpayer can represent himself or herself in court, although going to a federal district court, U.S. Tax Court, or Claims Court without a lawyer is discouraged. The Small Claims Division of the U.S. Tax Court is the likely avenue for a taxpayer who does not want to retain an attorney.

There are other important considerations in choosing the court in which to bring a tax case. Perhaps most important is the attitude of a particular court as expressed in its prior decisions on similar fact situations. You may want to consult a skilled tax attorney to determine the court in which you are most likely to obtain satisfaction. The following points should also be considered:

1. Tax Court judges are more experienced in tax matters than judges in the district courts or Claims Court; the latter must be familiar with many subjects other than taxation.
2. Trial by jury is available only in the federal district courts. Often used in criminal tax cases, jury trials are becoming more common in civil tax cases.
3. The court that will hear an appeal.
4. Discovery and evidence procedures, which are different in different courts.

Settlements are frequently worked out between opposing parties before trial takes place. For many years, the United States did not reimburse taxpayers for court costs. But since 1966, court costs can be awarded to taxpayers who sue successfully (see Key 48). Legal expenses are strong inducements for both taxpayers and the government to settle tax controversies out of court.

Decisions of the Tax Court, district courts, and Court of Claims may be appealed to a higher court. From either the Tax Court or a district court, the next level of appeal is the U.S. circuit courts of appeal. The losing party there, whether the taxpayer or the government, can appeal to the U.S. Supreme Court. To appeal, file a petition for a *writ of certiorari,* a request of the Supreme Court to reexamine the findings of the inferior court. The Supreme Court need not hear the appeal, but it might if the issue has significant consequences for the tax-collection apparatus. If suit is brought originally in the Court of Claims, the appeals route is to a federal circuit court and then the Supreme Court.

44

SMALL CLAIMS DIVISION OF THE U.S. TAX COURT

If you have a dispute with the IRS in the income, estate, or gift tax areas that involves $10,000 or less, you may ask to have your case heard by the Small Claims Division of the U.S. Tax Court. The only time this court is apt to refuse a case is when the IRS objects. For example, the IRS may feel that the case involves an important tax policy question that should be heard under normal procedures.

The small claims procedure offers a number of advantages. First, there is less paperwork—you have only to complete a simple petition and briefly indicate the IRS's alleged errors. Second, since trials are held in about a hundred cities throughout the United States, the trial location may be close to your home. Third, trials are scheduled more frequently than in the regular Tax Court, so the time between the petition and the trial is usually short.

Fourth, strict rules of evidence do not apply: any evidence that the court thinks is of value is admissible. Fifth, the taxpayer need not file a brief. Sixth, since shorter opinions are written, decisions are handed down more quickly than are those in regular cases. Seventh, since neither briefs nor oral arguments are required and the procedures are rather simple, taxpayers can represent themselves or be represented by someone who is not a tax specialist.

There are also several major disadvantages to

having your case heard by the Small Claims Division. Decisions are final. If the government wins, the taxpayer cannot appeal. On the other hand, the government may not appeal if the taxpayer wins. Furthermore, decisions cannot be used as precedents in future cases.

How do you go about bringing suit in the Small Claims Division? The first step is to write the United States Tax Court, Box 70, Washington, DC 20044, and ask to be sent the forms and information to file under the Small Claims rules. The court will send a petition form along with a booklet that explains the procedures, rules, and instructions for filing. The original and two copies of the completed petition should be mailed to the Tax Court, with a $60 check made out to the "Treasurer of the United States" or "Clerk of the Court, U.S. Tax Court." The package must be postmarked less than ninety days from the date of the Notice of Deficiency.

45

THE IRS'S POSITION ON COURT DECISIONS AND TAX REGULATIONS

The IRS may announce agreement or disagreement with a particular Tax Court decision. It does not do so for Tax Court Memorandum decisions or for decisions of the district courts, the Claims Court, the circuit courts of appeal, or, of course, the Supreme Court. Such announcements are sometimes retracted or changed later.

Regulations hold more weight than rulings as support in a tax controversy. Congress has given the Treasury Department broad powers to "prescribe all needful rules and regulations for the enforcement of the Internal Revenue Code, including all those necessary by reason of any alternation of law in relation to internal revenue." Courts are reluctant to overturn regulations that represent the official interpretation of tax law. Tax regulations are carefully written and reviewed. Most of them are released first in the form of proposed regulations subject to public hearing and finally adopted in the form of Treasury Decisions (TDs). Regulations, proposed or final, are published in the *Federal Register* and are distributed widely by tax reporter services.

However, even tax regulations may be stricken down if, in the opinion of a court, they run contrary to law. Taxpayers can and should challenge a regulation that appears to go beyond the scope of the tax code. However, you should keep in mind that intentional disregard of regulations carries a penalty. In addition, interest is payable on any underpayment due to negligence or intentional disregard. See Key 28.

The ultimate authority in tax matters is the law, but rarely does the tax code provide a simple solution to a problem. Tax laws are complicated. Even after reading the regulations, which are supposed to explain and clarify, you may still find the law ambiguous. In fact, there are many situations for which no regulations exist.

Look for the intent of Congress in the congressional committee reports. Members of congressional committees frequently offer detailed comments about the purpose of the legislation. Hence, committee reports are extremely useful in helping to interpret tax legislation, especially before regulations are issued.

46

WEIGHT OF TAX AUTHORITY AND IRS REVOCATIONS

Tax experts and practitioners face the difficult task of evaluating the importance of various precedents. The task is difficult because the field of federal income taxation is interwoven with a myriad of administrative regulations, rulings, releases, and court decisions. Moreover, tax cases are heard in many separate jurisdictions throughout the country.

The principle of *stare decisis,* "let the decision stand," certainly continues to have validity: the courts—within limits—respect opinions of other courts. For example, a U.S. district court must follow Supreme Court decisions. See Key 43.

But there are many complications as well. One is the respect that a particular district court should give to the opinion of a court of appeals in another district. A similar problem is the attitude to be adopted by the U.S. Tax Court toward decisions of the federal courts in various districts and circuits. These conflicts frequently are the basis for a Supreme Court decision to hear a case. The Supreme Court hears many tax cases that have resulted in conflicting opinions in the appeals courts. However, the Court, unlike the courts of appeal, does not hear every appeal it is asked to hear; it exercises discretion.

Further, the IRS frequently adopts official positions at odds with one or more court decisions. The only court decisions the IRS *must* follow are those of the Supreme Court. If a taxpayer wins a case in Tax Court, the IRS will probably not appeal if the circuit court of appeals has taken a position contrary to that of the IRS.

The weight of authority to be given to administrative rulings and pronouncements depends largely upon the prospects of its retroactive withdrawal or alteration. The introduction to each issue of the *Internal Revenue Bulletin* reads:

It is policy . . . to publish . . . all substantive rulings necessary to promote a uniform application of the tax laws, including all rulings that supersede, revoke, modify, or amend any of those previously published in the Bulletin. All published rulings apply retroactively unless otherwise indicated.

As the IRS itself says:

A ruling, except to the extent incorporated in a closing agreement, may be revoked or modified at any time in the wise administration of the taxing statutes.

So a taxpayer's outrage over a retroactively amended IRS position may receive little judicial sympathy. The hard truth is summed up in a sentence from a recent opinion in one of these cases:

The Commissioner's rulings have only such force as Congress chooses to give them, and Congress has not given them the force of law.

47

HOW TO START RESEARCHING

Suppose the IRS proposes to disallow a deduction that you think is legitimate. How can you begin to research the matter? A good, inexpensive place to start is with IRS literature. Publication 17 (see Key 12) is particularly useful because of its broad scope. But keep in mind that in "gray areas" the IRS's stated position is usually the one that is in its own interest.

Next, use the *U.S. Master Tax Guide,* published by Commerce Clearing House, or the *Federal Tax Handbook,* published by Prentice-Hall. Both are revised annually, so be sure to use the edition that addresses the tax return under examination.

These sources provide answers to most questions, but if they don't answer yours, you'll need to do more intensive research. You'll probably have to consult a skilled tax practitioner—a tax attorney or a CPA, not a mere tax return preparer—with an extensive tax library. Or you may wish to do the research yourself. Here are some suggestions for conducting that research.

First, find a good library. Most major universities, especially those with law schools, have extensive reference materials on tax issues. One way to start is with the subject index of one of the multivolume loose-leaf services. The ones most widely used are Prentice-Hall's *Federal Taxes* and Commerce Clearing House's (CCH) *Standard Federal Tax Reporter.*

The subject index of the services shows the paragraph number of the topic you are researching. At the beginning of the indicated paragraph, read the Code section, the regulations, and the publisher's editorial comment (but do not assume that the comment is correct). Then read the digests of court cases and rulings. Finally, consult the "current matters" volume of the service you are using for the latest changes in tax law.

As you complete each step, list the Code section number, the regulation number, and the names and citations of each case and/or ruling that appears relevant. Next, read the full texts of these cases and rulings. Photocopy the most relevant cases. Finally, consult editions of the multivolume Prentice-Hall *Citator* for the relevant decisions or rulings to determine whether each case was subsequently appealed, distinguished (not followed in other cases), or overruled by the same court in another case. Commerce Clearing House has a one-volume citator. The history and current status of a decision also may be found in *Shepard's Citator*.

Other services that may be consulted are Bender's *Federal Tax Service, Tax Management Portfolios, Federal Tax Coordinator,* and *Rabkin and Johnson.* On especially difficult problems, particularly those involving history, consult Merten's *Law of Federal Income Taxation.*

There are many articles and books about taxation and audits. To find a particular subject, check Commerce Clearing House's *Federal Tax Articles* or the "Tax Articles" section of the Prentice-Hall tax service.

48

COLLECTING LITIGATION EXPENSES

A taxpayer who substantially prevails in an action brought by or against the United States in connection with any tax, interest, or penalty may recover reasonable administrative and/or litigation costs. These costs must be incurred after the earlier of (1) the date of the first notice of proposed deficiency (usually the 30-day letter) that allows the taxpayer an opportunity for review in the IRS Office of Appeals, or (2) the date of the Notice of Deficiency (90-day letter). Your net worth cannot have been greater than $2 million when the litigation began.

Reasonable administrative costs include:
1. any administrative fees or similar charges imposed by the IRS;
2. reasonable expenses of expert witnesses;
3. the reasonable cost of any study, analysis, engineering report, test, or project that is necessary for the preparation of the case; and
4. reasonable fees (generally not to exceed $75 per hour) paid or incurred for the services of a qualified representative.

You also may sue the federal government in federal district court for damages if, in connection with *the collection* of any federal tax, an IRS employee recklessly or intentionally disregards any federal law provision or any tax regulation. You may recover the costs of the action plus actual direct economic damages caused by the unlawful action (or inaction) of the IRS employee.

Any damages recoverable under the law are to be reduced to the extent that the damages could have been mitigated by the taxpayer. In addition, a judgment for damages may not be awarded unless the taxpayer has exhausted administrative remedies within the IRS. If the district court determines that the lawsuit is frivolous or groundless, it may impose a penalty of up to $10,000.

A taxpayer's right to sue is limited to reckless or intentional disregard in connection with the *collection of tax*. Grounds cannot be alleged reckless or intentional disregard in determining a tax, or negligence or carelessness by an IRS employee. The total of actual damages plus the costs of action recoverable may not exceed $100,000. You must begin your claim within two years after the date the right of action accrues.

You also have the right to sue the federal government in a federal district court (not the Tax Court) if any IRS employee knowingly or negligently fails to release a lien on your property as required by the Internal Revenue Code. See Key 35.

49

OFFERS IN COMPROMISE

When both the taxpayer and the IRS are unsure of the taxpayer's liability, ability to pay, or both, the taxpayer can submit an offer in compromise, which is a petition for a reduction in the tax. Equity or public policy considerations, individual hardship, and similar matters that don't directly affect liability or ability to pay are not grounds for compromise.

A taxpayer seeking to reduce a tax liability on the basis of unlikely collectibility must submit Form 433, Statement of Financial Condition, which requires a full description of the taxpayer's financial situation to permit the IRS to determine the maximum amount collectible.

The IRS considers any offer in compromise when criminal proceedings are not expected and analysis of the taxpayer's finances shows that immediate collection of the tax owed is not realistic. Other factors that may lead the IRS to accept a compromise are the following:

- Sale of taxpayer's assets and payments from present and future income will not result in full payment of tax owed.
- A nonliable spouse has property that he/she may use to get a compromise of the spouse's tax debt.
- The taxpayer has an interest in assets against which collection action cannot be taken. For ex-

ample, the taxpayer owes a separate liability and has an interest in property held in "tenancy by the entirety" that cannot be reached because of state law. Under the compromise, the taxpayer offers to include these assets.
• The taxpayer has relatives or friends who are willing to help defray the tax debt.

The liability for income tax on a joint return is considered "joint and several." This means that either or both spouses are liable for the entire amount of tax. When the liability of both parties is to be compromised, the offer must be prepared and signed by both spouses. Cases in which a spouse was relieved of liability are rare.

Offers in compromise are reviewed by the IRS's Special Procedures Function (SPF). SPF may consult with the appropriate IRS officer to obtain additional financial information. When the compromise is due to collectibility doubts, the IRS will turn to a collection specialist in the field. But if there is doubt as to the liability, the matter is usually turned over to the IRS's Examination Division.

Rejection by SPF can be on grounds that the offer is frivolous, was filed merely to delay collection, or exhibits no basis for compromise. The following is a list of the most common reasons for rejection:
• The taxpayer has more equity in assets subject to the federal tax lien than the total tax liability.
• Total liability is large, but the taxpayer offers a minimal sum well below his or her equity and earnings potential (e.g., offering $100 to compromise a $50,000 tax liability). Although a taxpayer could be persuaded to raise the offer, the fact that the initial offer was so low indicates bad faith to the IRS.

- The taxpayer is not current in his/her filing of taxpayer requirements for periods not included in the offer.
- The taxpayer refuses to submit a complete financial statement (Form 433).
- Acceptance of the offer would adversely affect the image of the government.
- The taxpayer has submitted a subsequent offer that is not much different from a previously rejected offer and the taxpayer's financial condition has not changed.
- In cases involving doubt as to liability for the 100 percent penalty, the liability is clearly established and the taxpayer has offered no new evidence of its validity.

QUESTIONS AND ANSWERS

I read a book that recommends protesting taxes by not filing a return. It said the income tax is unconstitutional. What should I do?

File a tax return. The income tax is constitutional—the book is wrong.

I'm afraid I'll owe money but have none to pay taxes. What should I do?

File the tax return on time (or file for an extension). You'll be billed for the debt plus interest. Try to work out a payment arrangement with the IRS.

I hear that a lot of people cheat. Cheaters cause other people, including me, to pay more. How can I cheat a little to pay less, like others?

Don't cheat. The penalties are severe. Find legitimate ways to reduce your taxes.

Such as?

Retirement accounts including Keogh plans, tax-deferred annuities, and IRAs if you qualify. Besides reducing your tax bill, you'll be putting aside money for retirement. Series EE bonds for your children may save money.

Interest is tax deductible on home mortgage loans up to $1 million of cost, plus equity loans up to $100,000 above original indebtedness. Real estate investments that offer depreciation, charitable contributions, and many other items are deductible. Several books describe tax-saving opportunities. Check at your local bookstore or library.

I have been selected by the IRS for audit. What are the major causes of my being audited and how can I avoid audits in the future?

The DIF program (see Key 21) could have generated a high numerical score for your tax return. Perhaps there was something abnormal about your tax return, such as a deduction that seemed excessive for your income level, an apparent inconsistency within the return, or an unusually large refund claim.

Another likely trigger of an audit is the IRS's Document Matching Program. If you receive a 1099 form, the government gets a copy and matches it with your return. If it's not on your return or you didn't file a tax return, the IRS wants an explanation.

If you deal in a "targeted" item, your chance of selection for audit is high. The IRS has a list of targets—drug dealers, self-employed who may be tempted to hide some income, those with tax shelters, anyone with a home office, and even waiters and waitresses (many of whom underreport tip income) may be targeted.

About 56,000 tax returns are selected at random every three years for the IRS to measure taxpayer compliance. In this program, being selected for audit is just a matter of bad luck.

Other ways the IRS selects taxpayers for audit include tips from informers, amended returns, and business associations with taxpayers whom the IRS audits.

There is no surefire way to avoid an audit. Your

chances are probably reduced if you file a professionally prepared complete return. Add a brief explanation or some form of documentation for anything that may seem unusual. File the return and pay on time.

What if a seemingly abnormal item on the tax return is true? We bought an expensive home the year before the audit year and took out an enormous mortgage. Then my business soured and the creek in our backyard overflowed and flooded our house. We lived off savings from prior years. Meanwhile, my tax return showed little income, and large deductions for home mortgage interest, real estate taxes, and a casualty loss.

With any luck, your business records will be adequate to speak for themselves on audit. Substantiating the mortgage interest and real estate taxes should not be a problem. You should have some evidence of the flood situation—photos, newspaper articles, and valuation and damage estimates.

What should I do if I get an audit notice?

First, don't panic. Being audited is considered one of the most stressful events of one's life—right up there with getting a divorce, being fired from a job, or the death of a close relative. An audit is not life-threatening; so take it seriously, but don't let it depress you.

Second, read the notice carefully. Determine what issue(s) are involved and for which year. Does the IRS want you to mail in supporting documents, or to come in person to their office? Will they visit your home or business?

Third, are your records and supporting documents easily accessible? Are they properly organized? Go into your attic, closet, or file cabinet to find your reports, receipts, paid checks, diaries, etc., for the year in question.

Fourth, if a professional (CPA, enrolled agent) prepared your return, let them know what you received from the IRS. Give them time to respond. They could discover an IRS error.

Fifth, you're probably a busy person with lots of other problems on your mind. Think about whether to give in to the IRS, tackle the problem yourself, or get help. If the IRS is right, follow instructions and send in your check. If they appear wrong but it is a small item that appears to be resolvable by mail, do it yourself. Be practical. You might give in when the amount is trivial or when the choice is to become aggravated by fighting with a computer for an extended time period.

My notice wants me to pay only $276. That seems pretty reasonable for something I don't understand. Should I just pay it?

No! Most people would scream if anyone else sent them a bill for another $276—or any amount—that they don't understand or don't think they owe. But the same people just surrender to an IRS bill. Find out what it is for and whether you really owe it before paying.

When I correspond with the IRS, should I use the phone or mail?

Use registered or certified mail, return receipt requested. Attach photocopies of documents; never send originals. Unless you have a specific person's name and number, phoning will probably be frustrating.

When the amount is not trivial, should you handle an IRS examination yourself?

Probably not. Henry Inselberg, in a newsletter from Executive Reports Corporation, argues that a taxpayer should have counsel. Here are his arguments:

> Would you attempt to extract one of your own teeth or remove your tonsils by yourself? I shouldn't think so. You'd use a professional trained in the particular field. Likewise, you'd hardly attempt to provide your own defense in a court of law even though, in most jurisdictions, you legally may.
>
> Taxation is a highly complicated technical field. The Revenue Agent is your adversary to the same extent that the plaintiff or defendant is your adversary in litigation. The Revenue Agent is a highly trained individual and taxation is his specialty. Accordingly, your best means of assuring the most favorable outcome is to engage the services of a trained tax practitioner.
>
> In cases where one had prepared your return originally, call him into the picture. He's the most logical one to retain. The rules governing practice before the Revenue Service make him acceptable for the purpose. If he's not available or if you're not satisfied, ask your banker or attorney to suggest someone whom they would use in similar circumstances.
>
> A professional representative will not become emotionally involved as you might. He'll know how to get to the heart of the question, meeting with the revenue agent on an equal basis. He can be objective—you cannot. More than likely he will receive from you a power of

attorney authorizing him to act in your behalf. This will enable him to appear in your stead—meaning that it's entirely probable you'll be requested to go about your affairs while he meets with the agent.

There are reasons for this—when individuals sometimes get the impression that their integrity and honesty are being questioned they tend to become indignant, and sometimes pugnacious, thereby antagonizing the Revenue Agent. Or sometimes, they get overfriendly, suffer severe attacks of "foot-in-mouth" disease, and thoroughly complicate what would otherwise have been a very simple problem.

The experienced tax practitioner can ascertain the issues and reconstruct the taxpayer's records in adequate form. He can prove or disprove a Revenue Agent's findings since he is working at this type of matter frequently.

Should I give a power of attorney (POA) to my practitioner?

Yes, provided you feel comfortable with your practitioner's integrity and competence. If there is doubt, don't.

Does a power of attorney need to be on file in order for information to be provided by a third party to the IRS?

The IRS believes that, within limits, no POA is needed to accept information regarding taxpayer accounts from practitioners. There are exceptions to this policy that apply to requests to stop penalties or reduce tax, but these requests must still be accompanied by a taxpayer's signature or a POA on file.

However, this policy is relatively recent, and this practice may not be consistent. It must be remembered that IRS examiners are trained and reminded almost daily to scrupulously protect taxpayer information. When they perceive that a contact with an unestablished representative may disclose taxpayer information, their inclination is to be protective of the account data.

Does the IRS agree that a POA should not be required when the practitioner submits information and asks the IRS to respond to his or her client?

The current policy is to proceed on correspondence when information is submitted by a third party unless it is a request for abatement of penalties. Then, the IRS responds to the client directly. There may be cases in which the IRS may refuse to do so because no POA was on file; however, examiners are told that receipt of information or requests to contact taxpayers should be honored.

What is the difference between Form 870 and Form 870AD?

Form 870 is entitled "Waiver of Restriction on Assessment and Collection of Deficiency in Tax and Acceptance of Overassessment." It is usually used after the revenue agent's examination of a tax return. If the examination results in a tax deficiency, and you agree to pay, signing the form relieves the government of having to follow assessment procedures before sending a bill. For you, interest on the deficiency stops accruing thirty days after the Form 870 is signed. Form 870 is not a closing agreement for final settlement of the issues involved. The government can still seek more taxes later, and you are still allowed to file a claim for refund.

Form 870AD is a similar waiver form, but it is often used after a settlement has been reached at the Appeals Office level. Unlike Form 870, 870AD does not always stop the interest from accruing, and it requires a signature on behalf of the commissioner to be effective. Form 870AD also says it bars refund claims by the taxpayer, but court decisions in recent years have questioned the legality of this statement. Form 870AD is frequently modified to fit the particular case for which it is being used, and taxpayers should be careful to understand fully the terms of the document, especially when amended.

Are IRS agents paid a commission?

No. Supposedly, they are not evaluated on how much money they find owed to the government, but rather on time spent on a case. Still, finding plenty of additional taxes due can't hurt an agent's career.

Are there any controls over IRS personnel?

Yes. The Internal Security Division conducts investigations and examinations to uncover criminal misconduct and serious administrative misconduct by IRS employees. This same group investigates attempted bribery of IRS employees and any threats or assaults against them.

A taxpayer may sue the government for up to $100,000 for damages suffered by an IRS agent's reckless disregard of tax law or regulations.

GLOSSARY

Accounting records books of account, other records, and data necessary to support a tax return.

Accuracy-related penalty a 20 percent penalty to an item on a tax return that violates any of several different rules.

Acquiescence the IRS commissioner's agreement with or endorsement of a Tax Court decision.

Activity code a number added by an IRS service center to tax returns that identifies type of return (e.g., individual or corporate) and type of schedule.

AFTR abbreviation for the Prentice-Hall tax case reporter, called *American Federal Tax Report.*

Alternative minimum tax a tax to ensure that wealthy taxpayers pay at least some tax, regardless of their deductions.

Appeals officer an IRS employee who has authority to resolve disputes with a taxpayer, including reaching a compromise.

Assessment a bookkeeping record of a tax liability in an IRS office.

At-risk rules tax provisions that limit the amount of tax losses an investor can deduct. The limit is generally the extent that the investor stands to lose.

Circular 230 an IRS publication that sets forth the requirements and responsibilities of professional preparers of tax returns. The statement details educational, ethical, and procedural guidelines.

Citator a research resource that presents the judicial history of a court decision and traces subsequent references to the decision.

Civil penalty a fine or sanction against a taxpayer or tax preparer for failure to comply with tax rules.

Claims Court a Washington, D.C.–based trial-level court in which a taxpayer may sue the government for a refund of overpaid taxes.

Classifier an IRS auditor or agent who reviews computer-selected tax returns to eliminate those that are not audit material.

Closing agreement a conclusive agreement between a taxpayer and the IRS as to the tax owed for a taxable period.

Code Internal Revenue Code.

Collection Division the part of the IRS responsible for the collection of taxes, penalties, and interest resulting from the assessment of tax liability.

Correspondence audit an examination of a tax return that is conducted largely by telephone or mail, usually involving few substantiations or explanations.

Criminal Investigation Division the part of the IRS that conducts tax audits when criminal fraud is suspected.

Criminal offense as pertains to income tax matters, a willful attempt in any manner to evade or defeat a tax.

Criminal penalty a severe sanction against a taxpayer, as contrasted with a civil sanction. The IRS must prove intent on the part of the taxpayer.

Discriminant Function Formula (DIF) the IRS's primary method of selecting tax returns for audit. The DIF is used to rank tax returns based upon characteristics that are likely to generate more tax revenue.

District director the chief operating officer of one of the IRS's districts; reports to the appropriate regional commissioner.

Document locator number a number stamped on a tax return, check, or other document that allows the IRS to quickly identify and locate a particular document.

Enrolled agent someone other than a CPA or attorney who is qualified to practice before the IRS. Enrolled agents have passed a two-day examination or have worked in a technical area at the IRS for at least five years.

Examination Division the part of the IRS that selects returns for audit and conducts the audit itself.

Extractors IRS personnel who remove tax returns from envelopes and hand-sort them.

Field audit examination of a complex tax return by a revenue agent at the taxpayer's place of business.

Fraud a willful intent by a taxpayer to evade a tax. The IRS bears the burden of proof.

Information return a form filed to notify the IRS and the other party to a transaction; used for dividends, interest, sale of property, and others.

Internal Revenue Bulletin a weekly publication summarizing various IRS administrative rulings.

Internal Revenue Code collection of federal tax laws that have been passed by Congress. Known as the Internal Revenue Code of 1986.

Jeopardy assessment ability of the IRS to assess a tax immediately when it is believed collection of the tax could be jeopardized by delay.

Levy the IRS's power to collect taxes by distraint or seizure of a taxpayer's assets.

Memorandum decision a decision of the U.S. Tax Court that is often given less weight than a regular decision.

Net worth method an indirect method the IRS uses to determine the taxable income of a taxpayer. Increase or decrease in a person's net worth during the year, adjusted for nondeductible expenditures and nontaxable income, is presumed to be taxable income.

90-day letter a formal notice after an audit indicating that a proposed deficiency will be assessed unless the taxpayer files a petition with the U.S. Tax Court.

Notice of Deficiency 90-day letter.

No-change report a post-audit IRS statement declaring that no deficiency is proposed or no refund is allowed.

Nonacquiescence an IRS announcement that it will not follow a regular U.S. Tax Court decision.

No-show report a report written any time a taxpayer fails to provide the information or documentation requested by an auditor.

Offer in compromise a written proposal by a taxpayer to the IRS to compromise a tax liability based upon the taxpayer's inability to pay or belief that the IRS's view is in doubt.

Office audit an examination of a less-complex tax return by a tax auditor at an IRS office.

Ombudsman a member of the IRS commissioner's immediate staff who directs the IRS's problem resolution program.

Partnership an agreement between two or more associates to enter into business or to invest. A partnership is a flow-through entity that generally pays no taxes.

POA power of attorney.

Power of attorney a written authorization to represent another person in a matter—for example, before the IRS.

Preparer penalties fines and levies used by the IRS to encourage preparers and taxpayers to fulfill their responsibilities under the tax laws.

Primary authority the body of tax law issued by Congress, the Treasury Department, and IRS, and the federal courts. These carry greater weight than secondary sources.

Problem Resolution Program an IRS program that handles taxpayers' complaints and seeks to prevent future problems by identifying the cause of the complaints.

Regulations official interpretations of the Internal Revenue Code that have the force and effect of law.

Return Analysis Branch IRS service centers whose personnel review each tax return for accuracy and completeness.

Revenue ruling a substantive-type ruling dealing with specific facts and the IRS's interpretation of the law.

Schedule C the tax form schedule that a person uses for each business (or self-employed activity). Lists income less expenses.

Search warrant a document used by the IRS's Criminal Investigation Division to seize a taxpayer's property (e.g., business and personal books, records, legal documents, etc.) at a specified location.

Self-assessment the obligation of each person to determine whether he or she must file a tax return and pay a tax.

Small Claims Division a Tax Court division in which taxpayers whose disputed tax liability does not exceed $10,000 can try their case.

Special agent a member of the IRS's Criminal Investigation Division whose function is to develop criminal cases against taxpayers.

Specific lien charge against a certain piece of property making it a security for the payment of a debt (i.e., tax liability).

Statute of limitations the time period during which

the IRS may assess an additional tax or collect a tax *or* the taxpayer can file an amended return.

Substantial valuation overstatement 200 percent or more of the correct amount of value for property. A penalty applies.

Substantial valuation understatement 50 percent or less of the correct amount of value for property. A penalty applies.

Taxpayer Assistance Order (TAO) a binding order issued by a problem resolution officer when the IRS is causing or about to cause a significant hardship to a taxpayer. A TAO may order a stop to an IRS action or may require an action (e.g., issuance of a refund).

Taxpayer Compliance Measurement Program (TCMP) a line-by-line audit of the tax returns of approximately 50,000 taxpayers that is performed to gather data for use by the IRS to determine the best methods for selecting tax returns for audit and to evaluate the level of voluntary compliance.

Taxpayer any person subject to any U.S. internal revenue tax. In connection with the IRS and tax law, the term *person* includes an individual, a corporation, a partnership, a trust or estate, a joint-stock company, an association, or a syndicate, group, pool, joint venture, or other unincorporated organization or group.

Tax avoidance tax reduction methods permitted by law.

Tax evasion any method of reducing taxes not permitted by law. Carries heavy penalties. Involves deceit, subterfuge, camouflage, concealment, or an attempt to color or obscure events.

Tax lien a passive claim placed upon a taxpayer's property. Gives constructive notice to other creditors of a tax liability.

30-day letter a formal notice from the IRS giving the taxpayer thirty days to appeal the proposed finding of the revenue agent.

Willful a term used to describe an act undertaken with a bad purpose; without justifiable excuse; or stubbornly, obstinately, or perversely.

Writ of certiorari Supreme Court's answer to a request to hear an appeal of a lower court decision.

INDEX

137

BARRON'S BUSINESS KEYS Each "key" explains 50 important concepts and contains a glossary and index. Each book: Paperback, 160 pp., 4³/₁₆″ × 7″, $4.95, Can. $6.50. ISBN Prefix: 0-8120

Titles include:

Keys for Women Starting or Owning a Business (4609-9)
Keys to Buying and Owning a Home (4251-4)
Keys to Estate Planning and Trusts (4188-7)
Keys to Filing for Bankruptcy (4383-9)
Keys to Financing a College Education (4468-1)
Keys to Incorporating (3973-4)
Keys to Investing in Common Stocks (4291-3)
Keys to Investing in Corporate Bonds (4386-3)
Keys to Investing in Government Securities (4485-1)
Keys to Investing in Mutual Funds (4162-3)
Keys to Investing in Options and Futures (4481-9)
Keys to Investing in Real Estate (3928-9)
Keys to Mortgage Financing and Refinancing (4219-0)
Keys to Personal Financial Planning (4537-8)
Keys to Purchasing a Condo or a Co-op (4218-2)
Keys to Reading an Annual Report (3930-0)
Keys to Retirement Planning (4230-1)
Keys to Risks and Rewards of Penny Stocks (4300-6)
Keys to Saving Money on Income Taxes (4467-3)
Keys to Starting a Small Business (4487-8)
Keys to Surviving a Tax Audit (4513-0)
Keys to Understanding the Financial News (4206-9)
Keys to Understanding Securities (4229-8)

Books may be purchased at your bookstore, or by mail from Barron's. Enclose check or money order for total amount plus sales tax where applicable and 10% for postage and handling (minimum charge $1.75, Canada $2.00). Prices subject to change without notice.

Barron's Educational Series, Inc.
250 Wireless Blvd., Hauppauge, NY 11788
Call toll-free: 1-800-645-3476, in NY: 1-800-257-5729
In Canada: Georgetown Book Warehouse
34 Armstrong Ave., Georgetown, Ont. L7G 4R9
Call toll-free: 1-800-247-7160

More selected BARRON'S titles: